The Rise of the English Town, 1650–1850

New Studies in Economic and Social History

Edited for the Economic History Society by
Maurice Kirby
Lancaster University

This series, specially commissioned by the Economic History Society, provides a guide to the current interpretations of the key themes of economic and social history in which advances have recently been made or in which there has been significant debate.

In recent times economic and social history has been one of the most flourishing areas of historical study. This has mirrored the increasing relevance of the economic and social sciences both in a student's choice of career and in forming a society generally more aware of the importance of these issues in their everyday lives. Moreover specialist interests in business, agricultural and welfare history, for example, have themselves burgeoned and there has been an increased interest in the economic development of the wider world. Stimulating as these scholarly developments have been for the specialist, the rapid advance of the subject and the quantity of new publications make it difficult for the reader to gain an overview of particular topics, let alone the whole field.

New Studies in Economic and Social History is intended for students and their teachers. It is designed to introduce them to fresh topics and to enable them to keep abreast of recent writing and debates. All the books in the series are written by a recognised authority in the subject, and the arguments and issues are set out in a critical but unpartisan fashion. The aim of the series is to survey the current state of scholarship, rather than to provide a set of pre-packaged conclusions.

The series had been edited since its inception in 1968 by Professors M. W. Flinn, T. C. Smout and L. A. Clarkson and Dr Michael Sanderson, and is currently edited by Professor M. W. Kirby. From 1968 it was published by Macmillan as *Studies in Economic History*, and after 1974 as *Studies in Economic and Social History*. From 1995 *New Studies in Economic and Social History* has been published on behalf of the Economic History Society by Cambridge University Press. This new series includes some of the titles previously published by Macmillan as well as new titles, and reflects the ongoing development throughout the world of this rich seam of history.

For a full list of titles in print, please see the end of the book.

The Rise of the English Town, 1650–1850

Prepared for the Economic History Society by

Christopher Chalklin
formerly of Reading University

CAMBRIDGE
UNIVERSITY PRESS

PUBLISHED BY THE PRESS SYNDICATE OF THE UNIVERSITY OF CAMBRIDGE
The Pitt Building, Trumpington Street, Cambridge, United Kingdom

CAMBRIDGE UNIVERSITY PRESS
The Edinburgh Building, Cambridge, CB2 2RU, UK   www.cup.cam.ac.uk
40 West 20th Street, New York, NY 10011–4211, USA   www.cup.org
10 Stamford Road, Oakleigh, Melbourne 3166, Australia
Ruiz de Alarcón 13, 28014 Madrid, Spain

© The Economic History Society 2001

First published 2001

Printed in the United Kingdom at the University Press, Cambridge

Typeface 10/12½ pt Plantin   *System* 3B2   [CE]

A catalogue record for this book is available from the British Library

ISBN 0 521 66141 2 hardback
ISBN 0 521 66737 2 paperback

Contents

Preface

In the last three decades urban history has become an important branch of historical study. Following the example of agricultural history with *The Agrarian History of England and Wales* series and the *Agricultural History Review*, it has produced the journal *Urban History* and now *The Cambridge Urban History of Britain* in three volumes. Scholarly monographs and papers, some on individual towns and urban regions and others with national urban themes, have become numerous. These deal especially with social, economic, political or administrative history, or with a combination of these.

This book surveys the social and economic growth of towns between 1650 and 1850, drawing particularly on this huge recent literature. Controversial interpretations based on different approaches or research material are mentioned and the bibliography lists some 200 more important titles. The book follows the shorter *Decline and Growth in English Towns, 1400–1640* by A. Dyer in the series.

I taught a different version of this topic as a special subject for history students at Reading University for twenty-five years. Since 1968 I have published books and articles on the subject, especially, though not exclusively, on aspects of building. For this book I owe much over some years to the help of the former editor of the series, Dr Michael Sanderson, and recently to his successor Professor Maurice Kirby; to the thorough analysis of several anonymous referees; and to the care of the staff of Cambridge University Press.

1
The rise of urban England, 1650–1750

The network of towns in 1650

In the middle of the seventeenth century a rapidly growing London dominated urban England. Around 375,000 people lived in the City, Westminster, adjoining Middlesex parishes and Southwark in 1650, compared with 120,000 a century earlier [1:2]. In contrast there were between 600 and 750 provincial towns with from 400 to 20,000 people, nearly all expanding much more slowly [2:219–22].

Most important in the dominance of London was its control of inland trade. This was based on the use of the coast by shipping, and on its location near the mouth of one of the two most important navigable rivers and the inherited system of main roads which met there. London's manufacturing base, foreign trade and the growing demands of its own population helped to cement its place at the hub of domestic trade in foodstuffs, raw materials, fuel and industrial goods. Coal came by ship from Newcastle and some of it was distributed by water elsewhere in south-east England. Corn came overland, some of it from ports on the Thames and the south and east coasts. Luxury goods, either imported or made in London, were mainly sent on by packhorse or waggon. Dairy produce and textiles for finishing and export came by road and water, and livestock by land. London's importance in English foreign trade was still partly based on its position opposite northwest Europe. The biggest export, woollen cloth, went particularly to Holland and Germany, with Spain and Portugal as secondary outlets. London handled four-fifths of all imports, with most trade conducted by individuals or a few active partners, some of whom

1

were among the wealthiest City merchants. For example, the Levant Company was an association formed to secure favourable terms for traders, and the East India Company was a joint-stock company with single management [3:*24, 36, 41–5*].

Beier has emphasised London's role as the largest English manufacturing centre [4:*142*]. Cloth made in the West Country and other areas was dyed and finished in London; silk-weaving, sugar and tobacco-refining industries were created there by imports. Shipbuilding developed from waterborne trade. London's resident aristocracy, gentry and professionals bought London-made luxury goods such as jewellery, watches, stationery and books. Population growth and rising living standards among the upper and middle classes made house-building crucial. Although the City Corporation and about 90 guilds tried to control the crafts and trades, their position was weakened by the enormous extensions of building beyond the City walls. The Corporation and the guilds failed to stop retail trade by foreigners or limit handicrafts to those apprenticed and independent of a company. This relaxation may have encouraged economic growth to a small extent.

London was the seat of the court, Parliament and the lawcourts. The monarch's household and entourage numbered around 2,600 by 1640, and there may have been around 1,500 administrators [1:*12*]. The Inns of Court housed around 1,000 members. It was by far the greatest meeting-place of the landed classes, with several hundred residents, as well as annual and occasional visitors.

More than half of the provincial towns had a population of between 450 and 1,000, and at least 500 numbered fewer than 2,000. Market or country towns served a rural hinterland of between three and six miles. By 1650 even the smallest had a majority of craftsmen and traders, with a handful of professionals and perhaps several gentry families [5:*5*; 6:*1*]. Market towns were more numerous in the cereal-growing Midlands and the East than in the North, with its extensive heath and moorland. Traders often attended two or three markets within twelve or fifteen miles, especially those well known for a particular product. Towns on main roads were full of inns, and coastal centres had shipbuilding or fishing. In industrial areas townsmen not only sold food and other goods but also worked up and distributed raw material such as wool and bar iron, stored the finished product and dispatched it outside the region. While some historians have studied centres with populations of at least 2,000, the population – 5,230,000 in 1650 – was small and, except in London, sparsely distributed, so that urban functions are clear in centres with as few as 500 people [7:*257–71*; 8].

The majority of around fifty towns with populations ranging from 2,000 to 5,000 were small county, diocesan or subregional centres which influenced the trade of several neighbouring country towns [9; 10]. The markets in these centres handled more goods than those of the average centre, and were sometimes well known for selling local specialities. The larger traders were wholesalers as well as retailers, serving the grocers and mercers of the country towns and, at least in the South, the shopkeepers in the villages. There were also specialised retailers not usually found in the lesser towns, such as watchmakers, goldsmiths, vintners and stationers. The county towns had visiting and partly or wholly resident gentry, attracted by assizes, quarter sessions and the wide range of shops; and well-to-do clergymen inhabited the diocesan sees. The county and diocesan centre of Winchester had between thirty and forty lawyers, about 140 pupils at Winchester College, and canons living in rebuilt houses after the Restoration, according to Rosen [11:*170–84*].

A few larger towns were ports handling river, coastal and overseas trade. The rest served the industrial hinterland as well as engaging in manufacturing. While spasmodic efforts were made by corporations and guilds to control trades and crafts by insisting on apprenticeships or buying the right to trade and work, and inspecting manufactures, regulations were about to fall into disuse.

More than half of all townspeople lived in centres of more than 5,000 inhabitants [6:*90*; 2:*217*]. The majority were Londoners. There was less physical and working contact with the surrounding countryside. Around twenty-five larger towns had between 5,000 and 20,000 inhabitants. York and Chester, both county towns and diocesan sees, were regional centres. Ten towns, all county centres and some diocesan sees, had farming hinterlands which also engaged in manufacturing and fishing. Among them, textiles were important for Exeter, which also had a large seaborne trade [12], Colchester, Canterbury, Salisbury, Nottingham, Reading (which was dependent on traffic along the Rivers Thames and Kennet) [13:*53–74*], and Worcester and Shrewsbury, which both used the River Severn.

Ipswich men owned and built ships, especially for coastal trade, and Yarmouth was the largest fishing centre, particularly for herrings [14:*87–141*]. Both Oxford and Cambridge had celebrated university functions, as well as being county towns and Oxford a diocesan see. Coventry, Manchester, Leeds and Tiverton in Devon were mainly textile centres. Plymouth had a naval station and coastal trade, and Hull a growing river, coastal and overseas trade. With Exeter the largest provincial towns were Norwich, Bristol and Newcastle. Newcastle was the great coal port and the county centre of Northumberland, and had small coal-based industries. Besides its small industries, Bristol conducted the biggest foreign trade after London and dominated the inland commerce of the West near the mouth of the Severn. Norwich, the largest provincial town, was a county town and diocesan centre, and the seat of the East Anglian wool industry.

The urban hierarchy was becoming more integrated. By 1650 boroughs sent 425 members to Parliament, the central lawcourts were increasingly used by wealthy townsfolk, and the capital was emerging as a social centre for visiting peers and wealthy gentlemen who had close contacts with neighbouring county towns when resident on their country estates. Transport and financial services helped the growth of trade between towns. While regular carriers linked London with more than 200 provincial centres, payments and the provision of credit between different parts of England were made by inland bills of exchange on London, where goldsmiths and scriveners were also becoming bankers.

Compared to the English, fewer people in Wales, Scotland and Ireland lived in towns. This was because their standard of living was on average lower on account of poorer soil (except in Ireland), greater dependence on farming, and inadequate communications. In Ireland, a large peasantry rented tiny holdings. The largest Irish town was Dublin which numbered around 62,000 in 1700 and which dominated Ireland as the commercial, administrative and legal capital and seat of Parliament. The next largest town was Edinburgh, with about 50,000 people and similar functions. In contrast, in Wales, a largely mountainous country with no natural centre, the biggest town was Wrexham on the English border, with around 2,500 people. Welsh ports and county towns were dependent for trade on Bristol, Hereford,

Shrewsbury, Chester and later Liverpool, which added to these towns' economic importance. Around 17 per cent of English people lived in towns, and 7 per cent in London, in 1650. Although provincial centres had grown during the previous century, so had the rural population, and the largest were still much smaller than the largest elsewhere in western Europe. The phenomenal growth of London, faster than that of continental capitals, with an economy linked to north-west Europe, was the major reason for the rising number of townspeople within the English population.

Urban prosperity and change, 1650–1750

The century after 1650 was a critical time in the growth of London. By 1700 it had overtaken Paris to become the largest European city. While the total English population rose only slightly, the capital's population grew from around 375,000 to 650,000 in 1750, comprising 11 per cent of the total, compared with 2.5 per cent in Paris. London's domestic trade expanded enormously, helped by more navigable waterways and improvements to roads, on which waggons were replacing packhorses. Transport improvements were made necessary by the growth of London's own consumption, the collection of goods to be exported and the distribution of imports. Five great wholesale markets organised the sale of food to retailers, with a few factors increasingly handling corn, livestock, dairy goods and coal. Foreign trade was still dominated by London. West and East Indian commerce grew rapidly, and re-exports of sugar and tobacco were especially important in continental trade. London's foreign trade totalled £9.9 million in 1699–1700 and £14 million in 1752–4, or 75.8 and 69.8 per cent respectively of all English foreign and colonial trade. A quarter of the working population may have been connected with the port in 1700.

The City was becoming a financial centre. The Bank of England was founded in 1694, and private banks serving merchants in the City and visiting landowners in the West End emerged in the early eighteenth century. Dealing in stocks in the National Debt (created by the French Wars from 1689) and the big trading companies (including several new ones), the City was responsible for a Stock Exchange, with marine and fire insurance becoming active by the

1720s. Over a wider area luxury manufactures, such as watches (employing more than 5,000 people), jewellery, coaches and scientific instruments, were bigger and more intricate and varied. Porcelain workshops opened in the 1740s, and cabinet-making with mahogany grew. Silk manufacturing in Spitalfields, which employed about 12,000 weavers at its peak, was helped by French Huguenot refugees in the 1680s and subsequent tariffs against French silks. Dirty trades, many located south of the Thames, such as tallow-making, limeburning and dyeworks also flourished, with big concerns in brewing and distilling. After 1689 a London civil service of several thousand employees was created to meet the need for money in the Wars. The annual convening of Parliament from 1689, the presence of the Court, and improved main roads encouraged the further growth of a London winter season for the peers and gentry, who filled Westminster with their families and servants, spent lavishly on entertainments and luxury goods, and hired many of the numerous lawyers and doctors [15:*66–81*; 16; 17:*140–48*].

The hierarchy of provincial towns changed. The non-manufacturing country towns, district and regional centres developed slowly as the rural population they served ceased to grow. With rising farm and industrial output and general prosperity, inland and coastal trade and travel expanded, creating more town shops with a greater variety of goods and fostering middlemen, innkeepers, carriers, professionals and a few resident leisured families.

The development of a town culture, including classical architecture as houses were given brick façades, the layout of tree-lined walks and bowling greens, the arts such as drama and music, sports such as horse racing, and the quest for status and sociability among the more prosperous townspeople created an 'urban renaissance', in the words of Peter Borsay [18]. Weatherill shows that in bigger towns, and especially in London, the houses of the elite and middle orders became lavishly furnished and equipped for eating, drinking and sleeping to a greater extent than in farmhouses [19:*76–90*]. According to Estabrook, musical instruments, books, pictures, window curtains, mirrors, clocks and carved and japanned furniture were owned by the more prosperous Bristol people, whose lack of contact with country folk seems to partly explain why such consumption failed to penetrate the villages [20:*129–53*]. Towns became increasingly distinct from the countryside as crafts allied to farming, such as toolmaking and food-processing, became less dominant features. Populations of less than 2,000 grew on average by no more than 200 to 300, and bigger centres by 500 to 600. For example, the market town of Ormskirk in south-west Lancashire had 981 people in 1680 and 1,210 in 1754 [21:*xix*].

Rapid expansion occurred in a few ports with big coastal and overseas trade, and especially in the centres of industrial districts. By virtue of its commerce overseas, via the Severn, with South Wales and inland to the east, Bristol was the 'metropolis of the West,' according to Minchinton [22:*297–313*]. Liverpool and the smaller Whitehaven grew faster on the north-west coast, together handling coastal, Irish and American trade in sugar, tobacco, salt, coal, textiles, hardware and farm goods [23:*2–4*; 24:*393–402*]. In contrast, while Glasgow was the fourth west-coast port to import sugar and tobacco, it re-exported much of them to the Continent. Newcastle, and increasingly Sunderland, prospered from sending coal to London. Hull dominated the coastal and overseas trade of the industrial West Riding and part of the East Midlands.

Although manufacturing and towns grew together, the precise contribution of urban labour and consumption, and of the towns' collection of raw materials and distribution of finished goods for industrial growth, is debatable [25:*26*]. Textile manufacturing had varying influence on towns. Although the population of Tiverton, which made serges, fell sharply, and that of Exeter selling them and Colchester making bays declined a little because of marketing problems [26], other textile centres prospered. The start of silk-ribbon manufacture in Coventry, and an expanding framework-knitting industry in Nottingham and Leicester, brought great prosperity and growth [5:*21*; 27:*103, 122*; 28:*107–86*; 29:*96–8*]. Leeds made, finished and sold cheap cloths, and in the early eighteenth century began to trade in growing quantities of locally-made worsteds [30:*5–7*]. Manchester increasingly controlled linen-manufacturing in south-east Lancashire, finishing and selling the goods to merchants in London and elsewhere. The townspeople first made linenware and later cotton-linen cloth [31:*111–16*]. 'Norwich stuffs' continued to be made in what was now a wealthy corn-growing centre and still the largest provincial town [32:*263–310*].

On the eastern edge of the Black Country, a region of fast-growing metalware production, Birmingham was becoming dominant. Its ironmongers imported much of the area's bar iron and exported finished goods; its craftsmen concentrated on more specialised and expensive wares such as buttons, buckles and intricate brass goods, so that its 'Brumagem pretences' made it the 'toyshop of Europe'; the Snow Hill streets were the centre of the gunfinishing industry [33:*58–9*]. While Wolverhampton, which made buckles and locks, grew at a similar rate, Walsall, which made saddlers' ironmongery, developed more slowly [5:*12*; 34:*4–5*]. Sheffield prospered on cutlery and metal tools such as scissors and files in a smaller metal-producing district that was increasingly making its own steel, as Hey has shown [5:*12*; 35:*93–196*]. The populations of Birmingham and Sheffield sextupled between 1650 and 1750, faster even than the fastest-expanding textile towns, Manchester and Leeds.

In addition to the construction of large, heavily-armed ships for long-distance trade in London and Deptford, private shipbuilding brought more work to ports such as Newcastle and Whitby on the north-east coast, replacing Ipswich and other East Anglian towns because of lower costs [36:*62–70*]. The dockyard towns Deptford, Chatham, Portsmouth and Plymouth needed to be large because the huge size of the warships required a large workforce for their assembly; wars first with the Dutch and after 1689 with the French ensured these ports rapid growth.

Lastly, the market town of Bath was attracting prosperous health and pleasure-seeking visitors to its waters in ever-growing numbers, particularly from about 1700, as staying at inland spas for several weeks in the summer became increasingly fashionable among gentry and well-to-do traders and professional people [5:*1–17*; 15:*17–65*].

By 1750 around 25 per cent of England's population lived in towns, and 17–18 per cent lived in centres with more than 10,000 people. The latter figure was now higher than in continental countries (except Holland), where urban growth was much slower because agricultural productivity did not improve, according to E. A. Wrigley [37:*63*]. While London and the two leading provincial towns of 1650 continued to grow, the great provincial cities of the future now also emerged.

2

The expansion of English towns 1750–1850

London, county centres and market towns

With a population increase from 5,772,415 in 1751 to 16,736,084 in 1851 and a further rise in middle-class living standards, urban growth became more rapid after 1750. Features visible in the previous century sharpened. After a lull in the 1730s and 1740s, London's population grew to 948,040 in 1801. By 1810 it was nearly 50 per cent larger than Paris, and in 1821 Vienna had only 25 per cent and Berlin less than 16 per cent of London's 1,274,000 inhabitants. By 1851 the capital's population was 2,362,000, more than 13 per cent of that of all England and Wales [38:2]. The majority of towns were still centres in predominantly farming districts, and most grew only slightly faster than neighbouring villages. Again, industrial growth was the most important reason for the rapid expansion of a minority of towns. The further development of river, coastal and overseas trade and the new canal commerce caused the fast growth of a few ports. Bigger naval shipbuilding and the opening of numerous barracks in the 1790s and 1800s meant that defence industries increased the size of many towns. The desire for health and leisure was an equally important influence. While Bath and other inland spas catered now for residents as well as visitors, seaside resorts emerged in the middle of the eighteenth century.

London still had the greatest waterborne commerce in England, despite the rapid growth of Liverpool's trade. As late as 1800 it handled about 65 per cent of English overseas commerce. It had 25 per cent of British shipping and 33 per cent of British trade in 1850, using new docks of 1800–16 and 1828. In 1838,

1,093 weekly road carrying services left and entered London, compared with 493 in 1765. The growth of the import and distribution of foodstuffs was marked by the rebuilding of wholesale markets such as Smithfield and the Corn Exchange in the 1820s and 1830s. The new retail Farringdon and Hungerford markets were less successful because consumers used the many shops in the main streets, the larger shops having glass fronts and a spacious layout. Apart from numerous private banks in the City and West End, the business of the Bank of England grew greatly, and a new Stock Exchange appeared in 1804, symbolising the growth of the City as the world's leading financial centre, replacing Amsterdam as the centre of international finance in the 1780s and lending large sums abroad from 1815. As a manufacturing town London was now surpassed by others in the Midlands and the North. Its shoemaking was done partly in Northampton and hosiery had moved to the East Midlands, though silkweaving flourished until the prohibition of imports ended in 1826. Other specialised and luxury industries prospered. A few huge producers such as Whitbread and Truman and White handled brewing. Leather, felt and hatmaking continued south of the Thames. Because of the relative absence of government action the civil service grew slowly, though it worked more efficiently and departments were reorganised in the 1830s. Legal services had also improved by this time, and doctors were becoming more knowledgeable, although both professions expanded slowly. Politics and pleasure also brought more and more wealthy visitors to London, especially in the winter season [38:*46–82*, *158–201*, 17:*131–59*, *185–204*].

Better communications as a result of turnpike roads, canals from the 1760s and railways in the 1830s and 1840s strengthened district centres and many country towns. The wholesale function of shops and markets grew in the larger centres. Some small markets fell into disuse, and the commercial role of small towns where they had been held stagnated. According to H. and L. H. Mui, shops were most numerous per head of the population in the south-east [39:*295–7*]. Bigger stocks were held in more sophisticated premises, and specialist retailers now outnumbered producer- retailers. Shops benefited from McKendrick's 'consumer revolution' around 1750–75, when the middle orders copied the rich in a craze for novelties and changing fashions; though this tendency is particularly noticeable in these years, it also happened to a lesser extent in the decades before and after [40:*1–11*]. In the later eighteenth century provincial banking emerged, with 119 banks in England outside London in 1784, and more than 300 by 1800 [41:*6–7*]. Inns prospered from the growth of road traffic, the diversion of market trade to their storerooms, and the holding of a variety of meetings and social occasions [42:*91–137*]. Bigger markets continued in better premises and now used sampling for corn sales. Paving, lighting and the removal of street obstructions, achieved by commissioners levying rates, increased trade in large towns. Shops and amenities, and relatively cheap living, attracted more people of independent means almost everywhere, at least until the 1800s. These counted for around four per cent of the inhabitants in the later eighteenth century. Typically, towns remained in clusters, with an economic, social and administrative centre. Beverley, and to some extent the port of Hull, served the smaller, mainly market towns in the East Riding, while Colchester was at the centre of the baymaking and later principally market towns of north-east Essex [43:*100–2*; 44:*1–21*; 45:*111–28*].

Although the rural population was growing, the low standard of living of the labouring majority held back the expansion of demand and with it that of urban crafts, trades and services. Additional factors slowed the development of country towns after the end of the French Wars. Low farm prices between about 1815 and 1835 brought depression, especially in districts of ill-drained claylands where corn growing was relatively expensive, and even in areas with lighter soils more suitable for cereals, such as East Anglia. Towns were also hit by the competition of retailers and some professionals in villages, and the growing popularity of country houses among gentry families that had been town-dwellers in the previous century [6:*102–115*]. As late as 1851 many county centres had fewer than 20,000 people, and most country towns fewer than 5,000. In Lincolnshire, which was mainly agricultural, the county town totalled 17,536, Boston 14,733 and Louth 10,467, all helped especially by navigable water; four more towns had more than 5,000 people, including Grimsby, which had a new dock in the 1840s [46:*214*], and at least fifteen smaller settlements were probably urban. By the

1840s railways began to boost many farming towns. However, in size and rate of growth these were overshadowed by the industrial centres.

Manufacturing towns, ports and resorts

The pattern of manufacturing continued to change, and with it urbanisation. Textile industries declined or disappeared in East Anglia, the South and the West from the end of the eighteenth century, as much because of the competition of cheaper, often machine-made manufactures distributed by better transport as on account of the absence of coal. Towns became more dependent on agriculture; they included Norwich, Colchester and Canterbury in the east, Shrewsbury, and after 1825, the towns of North Wiltshire and Cotswold Gloucestershire. Their populations did not double between 1801 and 1851.

By contrast the textile towns of the East Midlands, the West Riding and south-east Lancashire grew between five and 15 times between 1750 and 1850, with Nottingham and Leicester expanding slowest and the Lancashire towns fastest. The hosiery industry grew during the century in the county towns of Nottingham and Leicester and in smaller neighbouring centres. There were about 8,000 knitting frames in 1727, 20,000 in 1782 and 29,588 in 1812. Nottingham also had a rising machine-made lace industry after about 1810, and Leicester began to benefit from shoemaking in the 1830s and 1840s. New hosiery types were introduced, and some of the knitting was put out to neighbouring villages [47:*1–104*; 29:*112–14, 166*]. As R.G. Wilson wrote, Leeds remained the supply, finishing and marketing centre of the West Riding woollen and worsted region. Flax, woollen and worsted mills were built from the 1790s, joined later by foundries, machine and other manufacturing works as the economy diversified [30:*90–97, 133*]. Halifax and Huddersfield were smaller wool centres but grew as fast. Bradford the centre of the worsted industry developed fastest, with factories from the 1800s.

Manchester dominated the cotton-manufacturing region. Its steam-powered spinning mills emerged in the 1790s; it supplied raw cotton and stored finished cloths for the whole manufacturing area and it increasingly bleached, printed and dyed cloths, and made dyes. Manchester distributed general and specialised goods unconnected with cotton to the region throughout the period, and later made paper and cotton machinery. The county town of Preston became dominated by cotton factories, and Blackburn, Bolton, Bury, Oldham and Wigan followed. In neighbouring Cheshire, silk was the basis of the economy of Stockport and Macclesfield until the 1820s. In Macclesfield machine silk-throwing began in the 1740s, and weaving was introduced about 1790. Though cotton largely replaced silk in Stockport from the 1820s, silk-throwing continued in Macclesfield, where the number of looms making handkerchiefs and other wares grew from 3,000 in 1823 to about 10,000 in 1840 [48:*113–44*]. Silk throwing from the early eighteenth century, then cotton and porcelain manufacture, also added to the economy of the rapidly growing county town of Derby.

The expansion of metal wares and pottery-making also led to rapid urbanisation. In the Black Country, Birmingham increasingly dominated as a service centre. According to Hopkins its small workshops multiplied with a more complex division of labour and technological change. Later, buckles declined, and machinery, steam engines and pin-making by children grew. Overtaken by Manchester in the 1790s, Birmingham remained the second largest manufacturing town [49:*25–80*]. Wolverhampton was next largest in the region, making locks, tools and furnishings, and other iron and brass wares. Sheffield made cutlery and tools, ivory wares and silver plate. In the Staffordshire pottery region, Stoke, Burslem, Hanley and Newcastle-under-Lyme emerged as sizeable towns. Coventry, producing silk ribbons and watches, and Worcester, engaged in glove and pottery-making, grew slowly before 1800, then more than doubled by 1851 [50:*49–75*]. In the early nineteenth century Coventry's weaving was done increasingly on power looms in factories, as well as on thousands of hand looms in cottages. Finally, abundant coal was responsible for glass-making and copper smelting at St Helens near Liverpool. Large-scale glass manufacture began in 1763 [51].

Defence industries also contributed to urban growth. This was most dramatic in the dockyard towns of Plymouth and Portsmouth, and the smaller town of Chatham, during the American War of Independence and the Napoleonic Wars. Peace brought slower expansion until their renewed growth in the 1840s and 1850s. During the war years between 1793 and 1806, garrisons housed in barracks were formed in towns over much of England, especially in the South. Although some were disbanded after 1815, they gave a temporary or permanent boost to urban economies [5:*44*; 10:*222–3*].

The rise of the inland and seaside resorts was another principal feature of urban growth between 1750 and 1850. Much history has been written on these towns in the last thirty years. Bath remained the largest spa [52], though in the early nineteenth century Tunbridge Wells, Leamington Spa and especially Cheltenham emerged as sizeable residential resorts [53:*111–312*; 54:*124–327*]. Bathing began at Margate, Scarborough, Weymouth and Brighton in the 1730s and 1740s. Brighton was the largest resort in 1801, along with Margate and Ramsgate [55; 56:*1–145*]. Between 1800 and 1850 Brighton grew exceptionally rapidly. At least twenty smaller sea resorts appeared in the early nineteenth century, especially in the south-east.

There are several reasons for the rise of these leisure towns. The middle class tripled in size between 1750 and 1850 as the population rose, and its wealth and standard of living increased as trade, manufacturing and the need for professional services expanded. The lengthening London and spa seasons provided the habit of holidays for health and diversion by the sea. While Cheltenham and Leamington served Birmingham, Weymouth and south-western resorts Bristol and Bath, and Buxton and Scarborough served Leeds and Sheffield, the south-eastern towns were primarily visited by Londoners. Coach transport became faster, more comfortable, more reliable and slightly cheaper. Sailing hoys were followed by steamships on the Thames.

With the great expansion of inter-regional and overseas trade, five major provincial seaports and trans-shipment centres continued to grow fast. Newcastle and Sunderland's coal exports, particularly to London, trebled between 1750 and 1830; both had small industries and Newcastle's importance as a regional centre grew. The population of both towns almost tripled between 1801 and 1851. Bristol grew relatively slowly in the later eighteenth century, but thereafter more rapidly. Besides shipbuilding, copper and brass works, glass-making and sugar refining, its overseas trade, especially with the Americas, expanded; its domestic water-borne trade was buoyant despite the diversion of barges and ships to Liverpool made necessary by the layout of the canals from the 1760s, and despite the growing freedom of the trade of South Wales ports [57:*11–40, 127–215*]. Liverpool was the fastest developing major port and, as Jackson has shown, Hull also expanded rapidly. The rapid growth of these two ports was due to their huge industrial hinterlands. Liverpool's comprised south-east Lancashire, Staffordshire and Birmingham, and Hull's included the West Riding, Derbyshire, Nottinghamshire, Manchester and Birmingham. Liverpool's greater size was caused by the faster growth of American commerce than European. The import of raw cotton was also crucial from the 1790s [23:*ch.3*]. Whaling was based in Hull from the 1780s, and both towns had port-related industries [58]. Yarmouth and Kings Lynn stagnated, while trade in Ipswich and Southampton increased by the end of the period [59].

By the early nineteenth century sharp regional differences had grown up. Towns grew slowly in East Anglia where Suffolk was hit by agricultural depression between the 1810s and 1830s, and in the south-west, where the Gloucestershire cloth industry was declining. They expanded fast in the West Riding, south-east Lancashire and the Black Country, which had neighbouring rural areas supplying migrants [6:*113–18*].

In comparison, English towns continued to urbanise at a faster pace than elsewhere in the British Isles. Although in Wales the new ironmaking town of Merthyr Tydfil had 43,000 people by 1851, the ports and inland towns were still partly under the commercial control of the neighbouring English centres. Dublin had expanded fast to about 200,000 in 1800. Only Scotland, where towns were now growing rapidly, rivalled English urbanisation in the early nineteenth century. The cotton, iron and machine manufacturing centre of Glasgow, with 345,000 inhabitants by 1851, was now much larger than Edinburgh.

London continued to dominate the English urban network throughout the century, although many manufacturing towns and the few large seaports grew at a faster rate. About 30 per cent of the population lived in towns of more than 2,500 people in 1800, and more than half in 1850. An urban nation began to emerge in the early nineteenth century, when the growth rate of towns in relation to the national population was faster than in the later eighteenth century [60:*3–10*].

The ties between London and provincial towns grew as inland trade and travel expanded. London banks supported country banks by providing credit and trading in stocks and shares for their customers. More visitors to and from London, an improved postal service, and London and provincial newspapers increased the flow of information. The capital's administrative, political and legal institutions also linked it with country towns. The resorts drew together prosperous townspeople from a wide area. The effect spas and seaside towns had on the economy of traditional social centres such as York, Chester, Shrewsbury and Canterbury by attracting their own county visitors from the 1810s and 1820s is evidence of their role in reducing local urban attitudes and prejudices.

Corfield and Wrigley [15:*96–8*; 61:*101–12*] have suggested that urban expansion stimulated both the English economy and population growth. The need for more food led to investment in the land to raise output and greater agricultural specialisation. Craftsmen and manufacturers in growing towns produced a wider range of goods which appealed not only to their own inhabitants but also, more slowly, to neighbouring farmers as links between town and country increased towards the end of the eighteenth century, helped by the development of suburbs around the bigger towns and the spread of Nonconformity in the countryside, if Bristol is typical [20:*12*]. The artisans drew on wool, iron, wood and coal from the countryside. Improved transport handled the increase in goods made and sold locally, and luxuries made elsewhere and abroad; in turn lower carriage costs increased deliveries.

Towns also supplied more services, such as grammar schools and academies; leisure activities such as plays, concerts, balls, and sports; and professions, such as medicine, law and banking. Towns increasingly spread new ideas, habits and expenditure by encouraging close contacts. Urban influences indirectly caused population growth through more employment, especially after 1750, and through the high degree of local mobility brought much of the demographic surplus into towns.

3
Some general aspects of urban life

Population: birth, marriage and death, and migration

The demographic growth of London and many provincial towns occurred despite a frequent deficit of births caused by deaths related to poor living conditions. Constant, sometimes large-scale, migration was needed to increase numbers.

At least two factors helped to improve the birth rate in towns. Throughout the eighteenth and nineteenth centuries, the vast majority of migrants were in their late teens and early twenties [62:*142*; 63:*28*]. Social mixing and working opportunities encouraged marriage and hence reproduction. On the other hand, London and large provincial towns had a higher proportion of live-in servants and apprentices (who could not marry) than did the countryside. Women made up the majority among migrants throughout the eighteenth century because of the demand for retailers, washerwomen, seamstresses and especially servants, and because of declining work on the land, particularly after about 1750 [62:*150*]. According to Sharlin, the death rate was higher among migrants because of their exposure to insanitary and cramped living conditions and diseases [64:*126–38*]. Most migrants lived alone in lodgings as they concentrated on establishing themselves in a craft or trade. As a result, the average age of marriage was later than might be expected in many English towns, as it was in Europe as a whole. However, as M. Anderson noted, late marriages were not typical of all urban centres in England. In the growing manufacturing areas of the early nineteenth century, such as the Lancashire cotton towns, early independence based on high wages led to younger marriages [65:*133–34*].

Table 1. *Mortality in London, 1675–1800*

Period	Approximate population	Death rate per thousand
1675–99	543,000	40
1725–49	602,000	45
1750–74	674,000	36
1775–99	814,000	30

In London, burials outnumbered baptisms through the later seventeenth and eighteenth centuries. Although the excess of deaths peaked in the 1730s and 1740s, and then fell from the 1750s, baptisms only outnumbered burials after 1800.

Earlier writers linked high mortality in London especially between 1720 and 1750 to excessive gin drinking, which weakened working adults and through them, the children born in these years [66:*41*]. More recent writers stress that gin selling was limited to a few districts and link deaths more to exceptionally virulent diseases such as smallpox and typhus [67:*72,121*]. Smallpox declined in the later eighteenth century, partly through inoculation, and after about 1800 through vaccination, though it remained a significant killer. From the 1780s the washing of cotton clothing helped to kill lice and reduce typhus.

The earlier writers also stressed the importance of a cleaner environment created by paving and scavenging, the building of hospitals and better medical knowledge [66]. However, urban improvements were limited to the main streets and the hospitals were few and only partly effective, so that these influences are unlikely to have been more than marginal. A recent attempt to link the demographic changes in London with fluctuations in construction, claims that the relative stagnation in house-building increased population density and hence exposure to infections in the mid-eighteenth century. This would appear invalid, however, because the high death rates appear in the 1730s and the building depression first in the 1740s [67:*86–8*].

Corfield has drawn attention to the evidence of baptisms, burials and death rates in the eighteenth century produced by J. D. Chambers and other scholars for some large provincial towns. Nottingham's population quadrupled, while that of Norwich increased by 25 per cent. The faster the population increase, the

Table 2. *The population of two large provincial towns in the eighteenth century*

Nottingham			
Date	Total population	Baptisms per thousand	Burials per thousand
1700	c. 7,000	31	30
1739	9,900	36	39
1775	17,771	35	29
1801	28,861	36	28
Norwich			
Date	Total population	Baptisms per thousand	Burials per thousand
1700	c. 31,000	30	34
1750	36,169	32	33
1786	41,051	28	28
1801	36,854	26	28

more likely that baptisms would outnumber burials because of the greater inflow of young adults. Thus baptisms in Nottingham outnumbered burials from the 1740s, when the population grew faster than it had earlier, and in Norwich burials generally outnumbered baptisms. As in London, the death rate in provincial towns tended to reach a peak from 1735–50, and to fall later in the century [15:*99–123*].

Urban death rates improved slightly in the early nineteenth century. In around 1840 official figures suggested a country death rate of around 18.2 per thousand and a town death-rate figure of 26.6 per thousand. Poorer families were largely responsible for the high rates. In Lancashire over 60 per cent of town labourers' children died before the age of five, compared with 20 per cent in more prosperous families, and death rates varied markedly between districts according to the incomes of their inhabitants. Among the killers were diarrhoea, smallpox, typhus, whooping cough, measles and especially tuberculosis, which was particularly potent among the working classes because of poor food and ill-ventilated dwellings. Cholera struck in 1832 and 1849, hitting the poor because of its link with inadequate drainage and polluted water [68:*101–2*; 69:*24–8*].

Migration was greatest into London throughout the period because of the city's size and deficit of births before 1800. Early in the eighteenth century at least 8,000 people entered annually. Although London drew on the whole country in the seventeenth century, during the course of the next century the Home Counties became the dominant source as migrants further afield moved increasingly to the rapidly growing provincial towns [15:69]. Between 50 and 65 per cent of the population in rapidly growing towns were not natives, including 50 per cent of the adults in Bolton, Manchester and Stockport, and 70 per cent at Preston in 1851 [69:39–40]. Provincial centres drew most migrants from within a thirty-mile radius.

Wealth, incomes and living standards

Several studies have shown the degree to which wealth was unevenly distributed in towns. The extremes between poverty and wealth were most marked in London, as the property of those who died between 1670 and 1730 shows. According to Earle, labourers left almost nothing, and £500 was the usual highest figure for artisans such as chandlers, coalmen, joiners and tailors. While smaller manufacturers and shopkeepers tended to own between £500 and £2,000, the larger manufacturers and retailers and some wholesalers, such as mercers, brewers and ironmongers, owned £2,000–£5,000, and wholesalers dominated the £5,000–£10,000 group. Established lawyers, doctors, senior clergy and officials left more than £2,000. Merchants and bankers, a few professionals and wealthy wholesalers left more than £10,000. The wealthiest townspeople in England were a few merchant princes with £100,000 or more. Rich businessmen and their families comprised around two per cent of Londoners; those above the artisan level comprised around 20 per cent [70:58–9; 71:34–6].

At the same time, in other towns up to 60 per cent of the inhabitants owned little or no wealth. The distribution of real property is not known, but personal estates of the more substantial minority are shown in surviving probate inventories. While most published collections relate to rural parishes, or combine town and country inventories, one relating to Rochester, Chatham and

Strood between 1687 and 1783 shows a pattern that is probably typical. Smaller estates predominate: 146 were worth up to £30, 166 between £31 and £100, 120 from £101 to £300, 75 between £301 and £1,000, and only 6 over £1,000. Tradesmen, including a vintner worth £1,034, were wealthier than craftsmen and more likely to be mayor of Rochester [72:*166,173*]. No-one owned more than £2,000. The contrast to London in terms of the number of wealthy inhabitants is marked. Although there were more affluent people in regional centres such as Norwich and York, their number and wealth were tiny compared with those of London merchants and other residents [73:*220–34*].

Annual incomes for the different occupations and social classes in the later eighteenth and early nineteenth centuries (when prices were higher) are known approximately [74:*42–3*]. In this period the middle classes benefited particularly. While manual workers earned £20 to £30, employer-craftsmen, retailers and professional men earned between £50 and £300 by the 1790s. An analysis by Schwarz of the incomes of the more prosperous third of London's population shows that all had incomes of at least £61, with more than half earning £79 or more, and ten per cent over £200. This made the last group the wealthiest two or three per cent of Londoners [70:*53–4*]. Presumably, they were merchants, bankers, a few manufacturers, lawyers, officials and other professionals, with some resident peers and gentry.

In England, between 1750 and 1850 the incomes of the predominantly urban professionals – solicitors, clergy, schoolmasters, clerks, surgeons, doctors, engineers and surveyors – tripled, though teachers' incomes were always comparatively much lower [75:*4*].

The standard of living of the lower orders has received considerable attention. Their real earnings improved between 1650 and 1750; a recent study by Woodward of urban building craftsmen and their labourers in the North confirms that the downward trend in food prices was accompanied by stable or rising wage rates [76:*13,177*]. On the other hand, the debate over living conditions in the later eighteenth and early nineteenth centuries has been controversial. It is now generally accepted that southern English real wage rates fell from around 1750 because of rising food prices and more abundant labour, and despite the fact that employment was rising, particularly in the 1780s and 1790s. After

1813–14 work declined with the return of peace but prices fell faster than wages. Real wages rose sharply during the next decade, then steadied until the end of the 1840s; poor harvests and high bread prices reduced domestic demand for manufactured goods in some years but these were counter-balanced by short prosperous phases.

This was the pattern for London bricklayers [70:*172–4*], and it was probably similar over much of the South. R. S. Neale described how the standard of living in Bath was up to 30 per cent lower between 1800 and 1815 than it had been in 1780. By 1832 it had recovered to the 1780 level. After further fluctuations, it was 50 per cent higher in the mid-1840s than it had been in 1780 [52:*282*]. Of course, these calculations depend on perceiving 1780 as a typical year; the leap in the 1840s is unusually large, perhaps reflecting a special local demand for labour.

Industrial workers in the Midlands and the North benefited from growing employment, real wages rising slightly in the later eighteenth century. Although there was a sharp rise in prices during the French Wars (1793–1815), the real wages of many workers were maintained. New spinning factories in the cotton-manufacturing region of south-east Lancashire provided work for women and children from the 1790s, while the standard of living of handloom weavers fell as the labour supply expanded too fast.

Views differ about changing conditions in Lancashire towns in the early nineteenth century. J. K. Walton notes that handloom weavers had shrinking earnings under competition from power-loom workers by the 1820s and 1830s. Mule spinners had short working lives, worked in unpleasant conditions and suffered bursts of unemployment, although a minority earned high wages in most years. Standards were worse in Liverpool than in Manchester because of unskilled, casual employment in the docks, the low earnings of women, and dearer housing. Walton believes that diet was often limited everywhere to bread, potatoes, tea and occasional meat [77:*166–81*]. On the other hand, Scola and others conclude that for the most part wages rose, prices fell, and food was abundant between 1820 and 1850 [78:*261*]. Economic historians such as Lindert, Williamson and Crafts, have emphasised a marked general improvement in the early nineteenth century among urban labourers, artisans, cotton spinners and coal miners in the North, and Feinstein concludes on the basis of evidence between 1780 and 1850 a betterment of only 15 per cent for the whole country Yet one should not overlook differences from town to town, between various types of worker in the same industry or craft, and years of depression and prosperity [79:*99–107*; 80:*625–52*].

Despite the lengthy debate about the lower orders, a steady rise in the prosperity of the remaining minority of townspeople throughout the period is not in dispute.

Means of livelihood

Urban local, national and overseas trade; and manufacturing, professional, leisure and defence facilities already influenced occupational structure in the seventeenth and eighteenth centuries. The variety of work, with more specialised trades and crafts in larger towns, was a basic feature of urban life. Although the sources for occupations are largely incomplete, and do not count those with more than one job, they suggest the great number and range of ways of earning a living in individual towns. Preston's growth as a service and leisure centre is shown by the appearance of doctors, and especially lawyers, among its burgesses in 1742 and 1762. There were also many more barbers, grocers and gardeners than in 1702 and 1722. According to Borsay the specialised trades included two printers, a bookbinder, bookseller, limner, nine tobacconists, a perukemaker, six staymakers, three collarmakers, three chandlers, and two fur-cutters. Like Preston, all towns had professional men, were dominated by trades and crafts and had few farmers. Many others had a larger manufacturing group of, for example, woollen or metal workers. Ports had numerous seamen and also some shipbuilders, and the small towns still had few specialised trades [81:*159–87*].

The early nineteenth-century censuses, especially that of 1851, allow a more exact analysis of urban occupations as Sheppard and Schwarz have shown for London. These were affected by economic blows inflicted after 1825, including the damage caused by the reduction of duties on silk on the previously flourishing Spitalfields silk industry, and by the availability of cheap Midland and Northern manufactured goods transported by rail from the

Table 3. *Occupations in Preston, 1702, 1722, 1742 and 1762*

Types of craft, trade or profession	Number of occupations
Textiles	35
Leather crafts	8
Metalwork	18
Construction	29
Food and drink	13
Carrying and transport	9
Services	14
Farming	2
Professional	13
Miscellaneous	17
Total	158

late 1830s [82]. Proliferating sweated labour often meant that women replaced men in some parts of the workforce. Seventy-one per cent (507,185) of employed males and 61 per cent (246,173) of working females appear in the census. Most numerous were the 18.6 per cent of males and 32.3 per cent of females working in clothing. Next were those in distribution and the 19.6 per cent of males, 14.7 per cent of females who worked in transport, which had risen since the seventeenth century, as the capital and port became bigger and wealthier, and the 14.3 per cent of males and 13.6 per cent of females who worked in victualling. Metal employment had fallen despite flourishing specialised crafts and the rise of engineering; only about 1 per cent of employed men and women worked in leather. Building, decorating and furnishing workers were slightly more numerous than previously, and civil servants and professional people had risen from 2 per cent in 1641 to about 10 per cent. The large numbers of women in domestic service, especially serving the resident gentry, professionals, and well-to-do traders and manufacturers, are not included in the figures. The other characteristic of London's occupations was the extent of small-scale production in small workshops and especially at home, which predominated in tailoring, dressmaking, shoes and furniture, and earlier in silkweaving. Nearly a quarter of English clothing workers were in London. Piece-rates were low and hours were longer than in the North for those in work in a surplus labour force [70:*242–5*; 38:*168–73*].

Census data for the larger provincial towns in the early nineteenth century show that county and regional centres with an agrarian hinterland, manufacturing towns, ports, dockyard towns and resorts all had different occupational structures. County towns in an agrarian district without a large industrial base, such as York, had numerous professionals and shopkeepers, a smaller leisured group and a substantial servant class [83:*96,195*]. In county towns and commercial centres in manufacturing districts, industrial workers were rivalled by craftsmen and tradesmen. Of a population of 60,642 in the county town of Leicester in 1851, 4,188 men and 1,979 women worked in hosiery, and 804 men and 589 women in footwear. Retailers and other craftsmen presumably predominated [29:*184*]. Manchester data show that major manufacturing centres had a commercial as well as an industrial function. The rateable value of cotton warehouses in 1815 was six times that of cotton factories. In 1841 there were more shoemakers and, perhaps, carpenters than male cotton spinners or handloom weavers: the warehouses were full of clerks and storemen, and the town, like the ports of Liverpool and Hull, had much casual employment [78:*21–3*].

Nevertheless, the medium-sized and rapidly growing manufacturing towns of Lancashire and the West Riding had a predominantly industrial occupational pattern. In 1841 between 50 and 60 per cent of the working populations of Ashton, Bolton, Oldham and Rochdale were engaged in textile-making and finishing. Bolton was also strong in cotton machinery and steam engines. The professional class was relatively small, the inhabitants partly relying on the professions and trades of Manchester [84:*154*].

With little manufacturing and an exceptionally large leisured group, the occupational structure in the resorts was completely different. At Bath in 1831 Neale has written that 14 per cent of the men lived on private means or were in the professions. Of the rest, almost 20 per cent were engaged in building, furniture and coachmaking, and another 20 per cent were shoemakers, tailors or clothmakers. Labourers were about the same number: nine per cent were in domestic service and the rest were other tradesmen and craftsmen. Women were still a clear majority of the population in the early nineteenth century. In 1851, out of a total of 12,266 working women, 7,751 were domestic servants, 1,436 were washerwomen and the rest were milliners, seamstresses and shoemakers. Domestic staff in Bath were particularly numerous, and those working in clothing and trades for prosperous residents and visitors were also significant [52:*268,276*].

Population density and social segregation

Town dwellers lived much closer together than rural inhabitants for several reasons. Tradespeople wished to occupy the town centre because main roads met there at the market place. By the seventeenth and eighteenth centuries, manual workers paying small rents were increasingly crammed into tenements, often in courts and alleys, and even into cellars. Later, a rising number of leisured people and wealthy merchants, manufacturers and professionals, who could travel to work, preferred property with large gardens and contact with the countryside. While this emerging characteristic reduced urban density, more plants and factories on the edge of some towns helped to increase it by the early nineteenth century.

Population density is difficult to measure. Towns which grew more rapidly before 1750, such as London and Bristol, seem to have been far more overcrowded than more slowly changing county and diocesan centres. Later, in 1773 Manchester and Salford appear to have had about 165 inhabitants an acre, based on 27,246 people living in 165 acres [85:101–3]. Figures for Leeds, provided by Rimmer, point to an increase from 275 people per acre in 1725 to 365 in 1770–1, 350–390 in 1780–1 and 341 in 1815, after which density may have fallen to under 200 by 1839. The higher figure for Leeds than for Manchester may represent a difference in the sources and method of calculation. In Leeds the pre-1780s increase was the result of intensive use of gardens and tenter grounds in central areas. Later, as building spread, and the Wilson Estate on the west side was developed for middle–class houses, density fell [86:*101–3*]. By the early nineteenth century almost all the large, rapidly growing towns had up to 300 people an acre living in the more numerous working-class districts, with much smaller densities only in areas of amply dispersed large houses [85:138].

Urban social segregation was based on differences of work, wealth and status. Some separation of various types of dwelling and places of work in the later seventeenth century is noticeable. Historians and geographers have analysed its extent, particularly in relation to the biggest towns. In 1695, according to Glass, 'London was an area with a fairly distinctive pre-industrial topography. The proportions of upper status households were higher in the centre . . . [of the City, with its wealthy merchants] . . . and the lower status households showed the greatest relative frequency on the periphery and in many of the parishes without the walls'. Elsewhere, as in Newcastle and Exeter, the prosperous areas adjoined the main roads radiating from the centre and strategic facilities such as a castle, church and guildhall or town hall, with poorer people forming a majority in the outskirts.

In riverside towns, waterfront streets gave access to waterborne trade and merchant families lived in adjoining houses. Langton's study of Newcastle also shows that the services and crafts tended to be segregated on the criterion of occupation, so that, for example, most butchers lived in one street and shipping trades were located near the river. Occupations were sited near each other to share facilities and sometimes wealth and labour, and to help suppliers and customers [87:*180–2,194–6*].

As towns grew during the eighteenth and early nineteenth centuries, segregation was encouraged by landowners and developers planning estates for larger houses or disposing of sites without restrictive covenants, which often created areas of densely packed tenements. Although by 1850 some social class mixing existed, the geographical features of urban society were changing more rapidly than before. The nineteenth century has attracted a few studies of larger towns which show considerable segregation by occupation, education and number of servants. Even in the 1860s and 1870s, the poorer trades were increasingly concentrated in East London, and individual crafts tended to be located in specific areas within and near the City [82:*6–7*]. In Wakefield in 1841, wealthier households lay chiefly to the north-west and south-east of the town centre [88: *211–13*].

As some wealthier families moved from the centre, away from

the bustle, noise and dirt of the business district, the older large dwellings near the centre were being divided. This area was joining the old periphery as a new core for the poorer majority to occupy and for use as business premises, run increasingly by non-residents who mostly commuted by bus [89:54–5].

4

The building of towns

Building materials, house construction and streets

Although the physical characteristics of house-building have always attracted architectural and social historians, the financial aspects have been a more recent study. This is partly because of the difficulty of generalising or obtaining sufficient detail from the sources, and partly because building lacked dramatic technical or even financial innovations. However, property ownership and lending drew on much of the savings of middle-class townspeople, and building was a major part of aggregate capital formation.

In stone-bearing areas the choice of building material was between timber and stone, with brick increasingly a possibility. Elsewhere, brick was gradually replacing timber between 1650 and 1750. Bricks and tiles were used by statute to rebuild houses after fires such as the Great Fire in the City in 1666, which destroyed 13,200 houses, St Pauls Cathedral and 87 parish churches, and many public buildings. The same applied in Northampton in 1675, when over 500 houses were burnt; in Bungay in 1688, costing £30,000, with only one street untouched; in Warwick in 1694, with losses perhaps over-estimated at £110,000; and in Blandford in 1732.

Bricks were fashionable. More town building in areas where woodland was disappearing and brick-earth was available made their use economic. Big houses were normally built with bricks by the 1690s, as was almost all tenement property by the mid-eighteenth century because it was cheap [90:*61–5*; 91]. As tiles or slates were also replacing thatch roofs, houses were more fire-resistant, warmer and more permanent, and they excluded rain, wind and vermin.

Between 1650 and 1750, the value of new tenements with one to three rooms, often in a group in a court or alley, was between £10 and £50 each. Medium-sized new dwellings with six to ten rooms and a street frontage in provincial towns cost between £150 and £500. The largest provincial town houses, which were double-fronted, and which had a basement and three storeys and at least twelve rooms, were often priced at between £800 and £1,200. Because wages in London were higher and the wealthiest residents were richer than those in provincial towns, some new houses in fashionable West End streets cost £3,000 or more.

Building and material costs grew slowly from the 1750s, and quickly in the 1790s and 1800s. House prices rose less quickly. Especially in London, there is evidence of weak foundations, bad bricks, thinner walls and inadequate timber floors, rafters and joints. Although costs fell in subsequent years, jerry-building may have been a permanent legacy.

From the 1780s back-to-back dwellings were typical in Nottingham and Leeds and were also common in Birmingham. In Nottingham they usually lay in rows, each with three rooms of 12 × 12 or 14 × 14 feet, with one room per floor. Their value when new was about £50 each. By the 1800s similar properties cost £60–£80. In Midland and Northern towns the price of new cottages of this size was steady at £70–£80 between 1820 and 1840. Tiny tenements in alleys and courts were put up almost everywhere behind houses fronting a street. Cellar dwellings were characteristic of Manchester and Liverpool. Whether the size of working-class tenements grew a little on average in the early nineteenth century is debatable. There is considerable evidence of one or two-roomed tenements in the 1830s and 1840s. The size of new artisan housing did not improve markedly until after 1850, when the building of cottages of two rooms on each of two storeys became frequent [92:*412, 427 passim*; 93: 94;*141*].

Substantial terraced houses of three storeys with basements and attics of up to 16 rooms fetched £800–£1,500 in Bath between 1740 and 1790, and £1,000–£3,000 in Liverpool in the 1800s and 1810s. By the 1830s detached or semi-detached villas of two or three storeys with nine or ten rooms in the spas of Tunbridge

Wells, Leamington and Cheltenham and the county town of Exeter cost between £500 and £1,500. Large inns, including 'superior' ones known as hotels, with up to 50 rooms cost several thousand pounds [92:*468–9*; 95: *386*; 96:*12–43, 114–52*].

In the absence of machinery, the scope for cost-saving in brickmaking was limited, although large-scale production near large towns encouraged minor technical changes. As Keith Hudson has written, compacting the clay by rollers began in 1741 and under a heavy weight in 1798. The use of wire to cut bricks began in 1841. Stone-cutting improved around 1800. The canals made possible the cheap distribution of Welsh slates, and their thinness compared with tiles made possible more slender roof timbers. Sawmilling by machine using horses began in London in the 1760s, and steampowered mills on the edge of the biggest towns in the early nineteenth century standardised production [97:*16, 18, 32*; 53:*117*; 98:*39*].

Technical changes improved the quality and lowered the cost of building at a time when its scale grew vastly [99:*231–46*; 100:*417*]. Revolutionary techniques in ironmaking, which became widespread by the 1790s, led to the use of cast-iron beams and columns, work on the Continent influencing English architects and builders. Concrete foundations were used in the Millbank Penitentiary and the British Museum after 1833.

The cost structure of house-building may be stated in general terms. The largest contributions were made by bricklayers, or masons in stonebuilding areas, and carpenters. Together, these made up at least 65 per cent of the total, with the rest made up of the plumbing, ironwork, glazing, plastering and painting. Although wages accounted for most of the cost of bricks, the charge for laying was small compared with their value. This was also the case with woodwork. Labour represented only 20–25 per cent of total building costs.

In house-building, a contract was sometimes given to a master craftsman who used up to eight apprentices, journeymen, and labourers in his own trade, and subcontracted the other work. Alternatively, the work was done by various craftsmen independently [5:*193–6*; 101:*10–16*]. The great expansion of demand for housing and public buildings between 1770 and 1820, and greater efficiency among architects and builders, led to changes in building organisation. In London the large builders James Burton and Alexander Copland, working between 1790 and 1820, sub-contracted to specialist craftsmen; from the 1820s Thomas Cubitt (who began by contracting for public buildings and then became the largest speculative house-builder) employed several hundred men in all the trades. The same type of builder emerged occasionally in large provincial towns. A large regular labour force enabled builders to improve the pace of work by careful organisation on the site.

As well as the ability to erect many houses simultaneously, great expenditure on many public buildings encouraged the partial reorganisation of the construction industry. The 1851 census shows the existence of some huge firms. Nineteen employers – nine in London – in England and Wales employed more than 200 workers. Three London undertakings had more than 350 employees. There were two more such firms in the provinces. Yet master craftsmen were still important, because of the need for repair work, alterations and contracts for a house or small block of artisan tenements. In 1851 half London's builders employed fewer than ten men [102; 103:*20–22*].

Our general knowledge of urban environmental conditions has developed from the 1922 study on improvement commissioners by Sidney and Beatrice Webb. Many more recent essays on individual towns have provided further information. The original pebbled town streets with a central gutter were the immemorial obligation of the householders: each had to pave to the middle. The custom was ineffective, depending on each householder's public spirit. Parish surveyors of the highways had a general responsibility. Sometimes manorial court leets, landlords such as corporations or charities holding considerable property, or wealthy private subscribers took action. Lighting of roads often depended on well-to-do householders hanging a lantern at their door. Roads were often narrowed by building encroachments. There were nuisances such as swinging signs, doors opening outwards, cellar flaps left open, steps and projecting spouts. Stationary coaches and waggons blocked the road, which was littered with piles of refuse. The town centres were congested with animals on market days.

After more than 20 by 1760, between 1763 and 1835 a great series of local Acts set up bodies of improvements commissioners with their own powers, and with the right to levy rates and to borrow on their security. They existed in boroughs and unincorporated towns all over England. A third were in the London district, mainly in developing areas, sometimes covering only a square and the adjoining streets. Many towns had several Acts extending powers. Westminster's streets were remodelled under Acts between 1762 and 1765. The commissioners replaced pebbles with squared granite blocks imported from Aberdeen and flagged the footways. This work was copied in the principal streets of some important towns. Even in Westminster it deteriorated because of technical weakness and the decline of local enthusiasm [104:*236–312*].

Expenditure on paving varied widely. In provincial towns a few thousand pounds was a common sum in the later eighteenth century, as in Southampton between 1770 and 1775. By 1800 the biggest towns were spending £10,000 or £20,000 per annum or more, as in Birmingham in the 1810s. The outlay of the wealthy Liverpool Corporation, which owned most of the town, was exceptional in the provinces: the opening and levelling of streets between 1773 and 1832 cost £645,891. Expenditure was greatest in London. The St Marylebone vestry spent £130,000 in the 1770s and 1780s on village roads and the new streets serving fashionable households [105:*6*; 33:*106–9*; 106:*133*].

Commissioners often tried to remove the nuisances at the front of buildings and to widen streets through expensive property purchases. Rates also paid for winter lighting, the periodic removal of householders' refuse in scavengers' carts, and for a nightly watch to protect life and property. However, the principal aim of improvement commissioners was greater comfort and convenience as business and living standards rose among master craftsmen, tradesmen, and professional and leisured townspeople [104:*254–5*].

The often inadequate and polluted water supply was also a growing problem, as J. A. Hassan has shown. Water was drawn from wells in back-yards and from road conduits linked to reservoirs, or was bought from carts. Larger houses drew water from pipes into cisterns or tanks from rivers or reservoirs run by private companies, which were common by 1851 [107:*98–102*; 108:*26–33*]. Water companies were joined by gas undertakings, the first being the London Gaslight and Coke Company in 1812. According to Falkus, by 1850 most towns with more than 2,500 people and some smaller centres had such companies, facilitating lighting roads and businesses, and by the 1840s many middle-class houses [109:*494–501*].

While middle-class housing conditions changed markedly, those of the majority only marginally improved. Their dwellings were still tiny, dark and unventilated, and contained little furniture. Although passage in the streets improved from the mid-eighteenth century, courts and alleys remained unlit, unpaved and dirty. Above all, sewerage was almost non-existent – a problem which was solved by one town after another in the later nineteenth century [68; 110; 92:*381–413*].

Land developers, house-builders and investment

Urban space was public, private and institutional: the first comprised roads and squares, the second sites for houses and individually-owned businesses, and the third locations of buildings and amenities held by institutions and associations. Most space was devoted to housing, which sometimes included work and retail premises, inn guest rooms, weavers' attics or sheds, and nail-makers' workshops.

In rapidly-growing towns most housing sites lay beyond the built-up area. Although building occurred on gardens, closes and the sites of old or burned houses near the town centre, as these plots became more valuable their supply became limited. The biggest redevelopment projects included the re-building of the City of London after the Great Fire, the remodelling of the centre of Bath by the Corporation after 1789, which cost more than £60,000, and the Regent Street scheme linking Marylebone Park with central London on the Crown Estate, which began in 1816 and for which loans of up to £600,000 were allowed [111; 112:*232–4*; 113]. On the edge of the town landlords or their agents planned and staked plots and new roads, then levelled, drained and sometimes paved and sewered. For big houses builders were attracted by large plots, wide roads and sometimes squares. Sites were usually plentiful because of the increase in value when fields were converted for building.

Landowners included corporations, chapters, bishops and charities; and above all individual peers and gentry, often with up to several hundred acres, who were frequently absentee; and prosperous townspeople typically holding no more than two fields. Some of the owners conveyed sites direct to builders, while others passed blocks of land to developers or promoters who then divided them up for building use. These men were usually successful building craftsmen, attorneys or surveyors. For example, attorneys were especially active at Spitalfields in East London in the early eighteenth century, and in Liverpool after 1800. For other townspeople, access to ample capital or credit seems to have been the principal reason for land and building speculation. This was the case with London's Thomas Neale (died 1699), master of the royal mint, East India trader and banker, among other occupations [114; 5:59; 115].

Land was sold for between 10 and 20 per cent of the value of the houses, or conveyed by various types of long lease. Selling was predominant in some towns, letting in others. Although local custom was a common influence in deciding the method of conveyance, large landowners and corporations preferred to preserve their estates for posterity by leasing.

Leasehold land was conveyed according to the type of dwellings intended. As the mass of the inhabitants could only afford the cheapest rents, most builders wanted to erect as many tenements as possible on the sites. The landlord was satisfied as long as the ground rent was paid. For houses fronting a road, intended for occupation by tradesmen and master craftsmen, the lease might stipulate a building of two or three storeys, and ban smelly or noisy work. In the case of large houses for merchants or professional men, who made up perhaps only 10 per cent of the total population except in the resorts, covenants often stipulated that the façade was designed according to the drawing of an elevation included in the lease or signed by the builder, and mentioned the type of quality of interior building materials [116:45–7]. Between 1774 and 1844 building in London was regulated by a statute which imposed precise measurements on four sizes of house [117:125–9].

The conversion of farmland into building plots increased its value by up to 12 times or more. If the landowner conveyed direct to the builders, he took all the profit. If developers handled the land, so that the original owner had no expenses, then he obtained around 35 per cent of the increase.

Surveying, staking the roads, pricing plots and occasionally designing houses incurred a small charge. Although landowners and promoters partly or wholly recovered the cost of levelling, paving and drainage as houses were erected, they initially had to do work costing by the 1800s, £200 or more per acre. Schemes were especially expensive when land was dedicated for wide streets and sites for churches, markets and squares. Money was sometimes lent to builders or the first houses erected to begin a project. In these cases expenditure of up to £20,000 an acre was common, most before returns from site sales. Some shrewd or fortunate promoters recovered many times the cost over five or ten years. Some schemes were abandoned because a local building boom ended, and there were bankruptcies and substantial losses, especially in the financial crises of 1793 and 1825–6. However, many other projects made at least a modest profit [5:*153–4*; 118:*13–14*; 119:*45*].

Housing, in the form of ownership or mortgage lending, was an important investment. Holding government stock and shares in the large trading companies was common practice in the capital and Home Counties through the eighteenth and nineteenth centuries. However, before about 1800 only gentry and wealthy merchants in the regions usually owned stocks and shares.

In London and some large provincial towns, for example Liverpool and Bath, most building owners were craftsmen. In Birmingham and Manchester this was not the case. As more craftsmen built to sell, in order to finance the next project, and the majority of non-craftsmen built to invest, the pattern of property-holding did not differ markedly. Local custom may have determined whether craftsmen worked on contract or on a speculative basis. For those without capital, materials were available on credit, and carcasses or completed houses were mortgaged or sold. In normal years, when there was a steady market, it is doubtful whether speculative building was much more risky than contracted building.

Most buyers and many builders of new houses aimed at a steady and reasonably secure income. Property owners expected a 6 or 7 per cent return. The gross yield on artisan tenements was 1–3 per cent higher, with repairs and maintenance, bad debts and periods of non-occupation accounting for the difference. Some scholars have condemned the profiteering at the expense of working men; J. L. and B. Hammond, in *The Town Labourer* (1917), complained of 'the avarice of the jerry-builder catering for the avarice of the capitalist', meaning the landlord. However, housing usually only gave a fair return on capital. Cramped living conditions were the inevitable result of low incomes without public or private help [120:*53*].

The occupational range of people attracted to building was especially wide in the industrial towns, according to Chalklin. Among site holders in Birmingham in the eighteenth century, those engaged in the area's dominant metal industry outnumbered both building craftsmen and general tradesmen and handicraft workers, and a handful of professionals and people of independent means. In London, craftsmen such as carpenters, bricklayers and masons made up the majority of building owners throughout the period [5:*170*; 121:*339–66*].

Building for long-term investment was characteristic of those outside the building trades. Although occupants moved more quickly, family ownership of houses for one or two generations was common. A few larger single dwellings were erected for owner-occupation, and sometimes the builder of a block of houses lived in one, or in a house nearby. Craftsmen were responsible for most houses sold within five years, while building for investment was part of the general habit of property-owning to let among the middle classes [5:*172–3*; 121:*294*].

Building societies based on the equitable trust first appeared during the 1770s in the manufacturing centres, as Chalklin, Beresford and other historians have shown. The law allowed more than six people to be members without forming a joint stock company. The trust provided its members with their own houses and dissolved when they were built and all debts paid. Paying subscriptions of several shillings a fortnight towards costs, members came from similar occupations. The charges put membership beyond the reach of journeymen and labourers. Societies enabled men with an income but no capital to buy property without a loan. Although overall the contribution of the societies to building was small, even in Birmingham and Leeds where many have been traced in years of great building activity, they went a little way towards satisfying the widespread demand to share in building. As a Birmingham resident noted in the 1780s, 'The itch for building is predominant: we dip our fingers into mortar almost as soon as into business' [5:*157–87*; 92:*477–92*; 123:*221–46*].

The wealthiest townspeople were not prominent as builders, despite their financial means. Local landowners, leading merchants, industrialists, shipowners and attorneys invested in rural land because of its social prestige; in banking, trade or industry, even in building land promotions, because of the potentially high returns; but only to a small extent, if at all, in housing. Factory and works owners in towns did not usually need to build cottages for their employees because the supply was already sufficient.

Very few craftsmen and long-term investors built houses on a large scale. According to Beresford, the largest builder in Leeds in the 1780s and 1790s was probably Richard Paley, a soap-maker, who developed 56 acres and owned 183 cottages in the town's East End in 1805. These cost him between about £5,000 and £10,000 to build [92:*215–19*; 124:*281–320*]. Those outside the building trades commonly took one site and erected one or two substantial dwellings or a block of working-class tenements. Steven Blake has shown that in Pittville in Cheltenham between 1825 and 1860, 208 houses were built by 119 people, of whom 74 were concerned with a single dwelling [119:*20*]. Thus expenditure was between a few hundred pounds and several thousand pounds.

The largest builders and owners were in London, where demand was greatest and large amounts of credit were easiest to find. According to Summerson, from about 1670 Nicholas Barbon was a speculative builder who was said to have spent £200,000, for which he needed to borrow sums of up to £40,000. He believed in 'great undertakings', seeing the advantages of mass production and standardisation in housing [117:*44–51*]. Another great figure much later was James Burton, who estimated in 1823 that he had built houses on the Bedford Estate worth £299,400 between 1798 and 1803; altogether in the years 1785–1823 he erected 2,366 houses worth £1,848,900. Hermione Hobhouse has described how, in the 1820s and 1830s, Thomas Cubitt created

Belgravia and Pimlico [125:*17–19*; 126]. Yet even in London the small craftsman-contractor spending £2,000 or £3,000 a year remained typical, with building owners outside the trade investing in one or two undertakings during their lives.

Short-term credit to builders was universal. Suppliers of materials, such as timber merchants, were an obvious source; other credit came from estate owners and developers. Men who handled money as a business, such as attorneys and later bankers, were increasingly important. Mortgages were important for speculating craftsmen when a sale had not been pre-arranged or was not immediate, and were used to a less extent by other building owners. Everywhere, general tradesmen and master craftsmen were numerous among the lenders, as were professional and leisured men and women. Mortgages attracted those wanting a secure, regular income rather than financial risk or the responsibility of managing property [5:*235–43*; 122:*294–5*; 119:*23*, *31*]. Overall, a huge number of local inhabitants of moderate means financed building in some way.

Public buildings, harbours, docks and factories

Alongside housing there was a small but growing expenditure on public buildings and churches, as they increased in number, type and even size. Public buildings found in country parishes as well as in towns, were generally larger in urban centres because of population size, and those serving districts or counties were usually in towns because of their location. Construction was exceptional in London because of its huge population, concentration of wealth, and role as the seat of the court, government departments, Parliament and lawcourts, and other major public buildings. Reconstruction after the Great Fire and the continental example played a special part in the later seventeenth century Particularly in provincial towns, outlay rose during the eighteenth century, with a sharp increase from the 1760s and 1770s which continued through the nineteenth century [127:*1–26*; 128].

The most expensive public buildings are listed in Table 4 (see below p. 42). Some public buildings erected in London and the provinces were paid for out of taxes or rates. Rates were responsible for county gaols, which cost a few thousand pounds if rebuilt between 1650 and 1750 and up to £200,000 in the early nineteenth century, and the more numerous and mostly smaller county houses of correction, shire halls, and after 1808, county pauper lunatic asylums. Parish levies rebuilt some churches for a few thousand pounds up to the 1780s, then for perhaps £10,000 or £15,000, and many hundred town workhouses from the 1720s for several hundred pounds and in the early nineteenth century up to £10,000 or £15,000.

Parliamentary taxation paid for new government buildings including Somerset House, the lawcourts in the early nineteenth century, the rebuilding of the Houses of Parliament after the fire of 1834, new churches for services to improve the morals and social discipline of the poor under the Acts of 1818 and 1824, and other important public buildings.

Taxes on coals brought into London paid for the churches and new public buildings in the City after the Great Fire, and twelve suburban churches between 1711 and 1740, and met much of the cost of Newgate Prison in the 1770s.

Private donations, and increasingly subscriptions by many well-to-do people, paid for the other public buildings. Town halls were built by corporations from estate income or presented as a gift from local Members of Parliament or landowners to court political popularity. The range and size of market structures grew, including special types such as cloth halls in the West Riding and merchants' exchanges in the largest ports. As the wealth and leisure of the upper and middle classes grew, suitable buildings for drama, dancing, card playing and conversation appeared, paid for by subscription. Throughout the eighteenth century and beyond theatres and structures for mixed entertainment were built in London. From the 1730s local gentry and prosperous townspeople in provincial centres tried to ape London with their own theatres and assembly rooms, initially costing up to £5,000, and from the 1790s up to £10,000. The largest London theatres cost much more, the most expensive being Drury Lane in 1811 for £150,000. More churches in expanding towns were erected through prosperous people buying or renting pews as church-going was fashionable. Collections paid for the thousands of Nonconformist chapels, typically costing £200 or £300 each, in the late eighteenth century, and up to a few thousand pounds from the 1810s. New university buildings – blocks of college rooms, libraries and chapels – were erected piecemeal in Oxford and Cambridge, and in London for the first time in the 1820s and 1830s. Nearly 200 grammar schools were erected between 1650 and 1800, older buildings being rebuilt or extended. Some large private schools were built in the early nineteenth century. Many hundreds of one-room charity schools were set up – to give the poor moral discipline as well as literacy – in towns in the early eighteenth century, and more from the 1810s, all supported by local subscriptions from the well-to-do. This benevolence was also responsible for hospitals for the poor, aimed at restoring them both to health and work. These began in London in the 1730s; in provincial towns 38 were erected on the London model between 1735 and 1800, for a few thousand pounds each. Almshouses for the elderly were still being built, including palace-like groups of buildings at Chelsea and Greenwich for retired and invalid soldiers and sailors at the end of the seventeenth century, based on the model of the Invalides in Paris (1670). Orphans were housed in the London Foundling Hospital erected in the 1740s. More hospitals were built everywhere in the early nineteenth century. Finally, from the 1810s and 1820s some libraries, newsrooms, lecture rooms and learned institutions were founded not only in London but in the largest provincial towns, such as Liverpool and Manchester, and in some county towns. London began opening its purpose-built gentlemen's clubs from the 1810s. The British Museum and National Gallery were built with funding from taxation.

There were also public works for military purposes. Naval dockyards were extended in Chatham and created in Portsmouth, Plymouth and Sheerness. Coastal fortifications were erected from the 1750s, for example at Dover Castle and around the dockyards at Chatham, Portsmouth and Plymouth. Several million pounds were spent on 155 barracks during the French Wars from 1793 to 1815.

By the 1820s, civilian public buildings, including churches and palaces, were absorbing more than 10 per cent of housing expenditure – more than a million pounds a year. While this was a part of the great urban expansion, changing social influences were also

Table 4. *Some of the largest public buildings, 1650–1850*

Date	Building	Cost (£)
1667–9	Royal Exchange, London	58,962
1667–71	Guildhall, London	36,498
c.1670–1700	St Paul's Cathedral	736,800
1680s–1700	Royal Hospital, Chelsea	more than 100,000
1694–1728	Royal Hospital for Seamen, Greenwich	c.200,000
1741	Rotunda, Ranelagh, London	c.36,000
1741–3	Bristol Exchange	almost 50,000
1742–4	Foundling Hospital	35,062 with site
1740s	Radcliffe Camera, Oxford	43,226
1769–76	Excise Office, London	39,339
1775–1801	Somerset House	462,323
1805–15	Royal Mint	288,656
1810–19	Kent County Gaol	c.200,000
1813–29	Custom House	435,000
1816–21	Millbank Prison, London	500,000
1819	General Post Office	499,000
1824–35	Windsor Castle	771,000
1825–30	Buckingham Palace	576,373
1826–37	Yorkshire County Gaol	203,000
1820s and 1830s	London University	c.200,000
1833	Hungerford Market, London	more than 200,000
1835–60	Houses of Parliament	2,400,000

It should be noted that building costs more than doubled between 1750 and 1810, followed by a slight fall.

important. Increasing humanitarianism at the end of the eighteenth century encouraged the building of larger prisons with individual cells and chapels as well as work rooms, and of pauper lunatic asylums in some counties. The growth of religious enthusiasm explains the growth of Anglican church building and the proliferation of Free Church and Methodist chapels from the 1810s.

Harbour construction expanded and dock building began between 1660 and 1760. While, typically, several thousand pounds were spent on piers and quays, the few earlier commercial docks were more expensive. Outlay on ports increased in the

1760s and 1770s, and especially from the 1790s. From £5,000 to £10,000 each in the 1760s, outlay reached at least £40,000 by the 1820s. For example the new pier at Whitehaven cost around £50,000 in 1823–32. Provincial dock-building was greatest at Liverpool, where the flow of the Mersey hindered the loading and unloading of ships at quays. According to Longmore, the Corporation spent between £15,000 and £25,000 each on five docks in the eighteenth century, and £650,000, £438,000 and £795,000 (excluding the land) on three enormous docks between 1816 and 1836, driving up port duties. Bristol built docks in the eighteenth century, Hull two from the 1770s and Southampton, Ipswich and Grimsby one each between 1838 and 1848. Above all, companies were responsible for five great London docks between 1800 and 1830, which cost between £375,000 and £3,350,000 [129:*33–9*: 130:*139–40*].

Mills to grind corn or make paper, iron furnaces and forges; and copper smelting works and brass mills driven by wind, horse or water power were run by a few skilled workers, and were located as easily in the country as in the town. Coal mines relied on large rural villages for labour. The first demand for at least several hundred male workers came from the naval shipyards of the seventeenth century; towns grew up to house the shipwrights. From the late seventeenth century large breweries, especially in London, some tanneries and, by the 1840s, engineering works employed scores of site workers.

In the growing textile industry of the Midlands and the North during the eighteenth and nineteenth centuries the availability of a sufficient supply of men, women and child workers was a main reason for the location of factories on the edge of towns; this factor, with easy access to sources of raw materials and to warehouses for the marketing of cloths, greatly outweighed the higher cost of building sites in a town. From 1717 silk-throwing mills were built in Derby, Macclesfield, Stockport and Manchester. Then, in the late 1770s and 1780s, water-powered cotton mills were erected both in the country and in towns. When steam power, used for cotton-spinning from the 1790s, especially in south-east Lancashire, and later for worsteds and woollens in the West Riding, made streams unnecessary, almost all mills were in towns. S. D. Chapman has suggested that there were 900 cotton mills in 1797, of which the building and machinery could cost up to £5,000. In the early nineteenth century, cotton factories grew in size rather than number, and several hundred men, women and child employees became typical. By the 1840s some 1,200 mills were worth £10,000–£15,000 each. At this time, factories were dominating worsted-making and beginning to take over woollens. Steam mills spread slowly to corn grinding, sawing and engineering. Although much manufacture and craftwork was still done at home or in small workshops, heavy investment in some ports and industrial towns from the 1780s and 1790s was steadily relocating the urban workforce into warehouses and factories [131:*28–42*].

Building and urban growth

Building activity changed by the year. The last century shows that the volume of investment fluctuates according to a cycle of eighteen or twenty years. A trough in building which lasts three or four years is followed by a recovery which reaches boom conditions eight or nine years later. Then construction falls gradually and building becomes depressed again. Builders take time to react to a changing market in the form of the number of empty properties and rent levels, and several months are needed for building decisions to become finished houses. Thus supply and demand are never matched. Rates of interest and the cost of materials during war and peace also affect supply. Periods of prosperity and depression, and the extent to which new households are created, influence demand.

These factors caused building fluctuations in the eighteenth and early nineteenth centuries, according to qualitative evidence and statistical series of imported softwoods from 1697, and brick output from 1785, and numbers of deeds registered in Middlesex and Yorkshire from the 1700s. As towns in aggregate grew faster than the rural population, the majority of new houses were in urban areas. [132:*14*; 133]. Other forms of building had a small influence. Public buildings were erected in periods of urban growth (when most houses were built). Factories and docks were a further response to urban prosperity, and railways affected brick

Table 5. *Building fluctuations, c.1700–1850*

Trough	Peak	Trough	Years between Peaks	Years between Troughs
c.1698?	1705?	c.1711	–	–
c.1711	1724	1729	19	18
1729	1736	1744	12	15
1744	1753	1762	17	18
1762	1776	1781	23	19
1781	1792	1799	16	18
1799	1811	1816	19	17
1816	1825	1832	14	16
1832	1836	1843	11	11
1843	1847	–	11	–

output in the 1840s. The figures suggest that there were six building peaks and six troughs in the eighteenth century, and four booms and four depressions between 1800 and 1850. H. A. Shannon and T. S. Ashton believe that brick output altered according to interest-rate changes because builders worked with credit, arguing that a change in the interest rate of half or 1 per cent was sufficient to encourage or deter builders. In fact, a 4 per cent rate did not raise the amount of building in some years, nor did a 5 per cent rate necessarily discourage it. It was the availability of credit, not its price, that was crucial in the mid-1790s, when credit was short and building declined, and in 1824–5, when it was plentiful and helped to cause a speculative boom [134; 135:*84–137*].

Parry Lewis has produced a demographic thesis. He argues that the high number of marriages and births over several years led to a housing demand, which was echoed around eighteen years later as the children began to earn and their own marriages brought more accommodation pressure [132:*10–60, 174, 186–94*; 5:*255, 297–8*]. Chalklin has presented further evidence for the provincial towns, linking the amount of building to local trading or industrial activity and demographic changes. While confidence and the speculative urge among builders were important, changes in population and prosperity were crucial. Following Chalklin, the most useful contribution has been that of Sheppard *et al*, giving statistics of all property conveyances relating to Middlesex (that is,

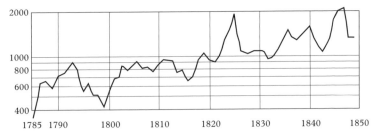

Figure 1. Annual output of bricks in England and Wales, 1785–1849 (in millions)

in effect, London) and the three Yorkshire Ridings as a substitute for building deeds. Further major changes in general interpretation are unlikely, though more material about local fluctuations is likely to emerge [5:*249–303*; 136:*176–217*].

Although the evidence is insufficient before 1800, the supply of housing probably kept up with population growth in the early nineteenth century. If one accepts a common definition of a house, the number of people per inhabited house varied between 5.76 and 5.44 in the six census years between 1801 and 1851. There were local differences, and sharp changes over time in individual streets and groups of courts and alleys. Rents were higher in the town than in the country, and seem to have risen as a percentage of urban working-class incomes between the later eighteenth century and the 1830s and 1840s, at least in London and Leeds. Some of the improvement in real wages after the end of the French Wars paid for higher rents [137:*14*; 138:*201, 211*; 70:*192–4*; 139; 5:*207*].

During each decade between 1791 and 1840 the number of new houses rose, from 223,000 in 1791–1800 to 685,000 in 1831–40, falling to 507,000 in 1841–50. Annual expenditure on houses and public buildings increased almost tenfold between 1761–1780 and 1821–1840, after which there was a decade of decline; the figure was around £1,500,000 in 1761–80 and around £10,000,000 in 1821–30 and almost £12,000,000 in 1831–40. While house-building grew between 1650 and 1750, despite occasional local booms and depressions, the fluctuations of the following century were accompanied by an almost dramatically rising trend [140:*40–1, 44*].

5

The elite and the middle orders: social background

Leisured people

Urban society comprised relatively few leisured people; a middle order or orders, who were mostly masters or employers and their families, of varied wealth, earnings and status, increasingly known from the later eighteenth century as the middle class or classes; and the lower order or orders, later the working class or classes, again with varied incomes, which included the great majority of inhabitants.

All towns had a few retired tradesmen and professionals along with widows and unmarried women of independent means, as well as members of the gentry who owned neighbouring landed estates and who lived in the largest houses, and the younger sons and daughters of gentlemen, who were also economically inactive. They were attracted by the leisured company and modest living, together with the prosperity of the town, as shown by its shops and entertainments. In 1650 no more than 1 or 2 per cent of families in most towns were leisured. Some larger towns, such as county and diocesan centres, became notable as gentry residences. Fiennes wrote in 1698 of an 'abundance of people of quality [living] in Shrewsbury more than in any town except Nottingham' [141:*186*]. By 1800 the percentage of leisured families was between 3 and 5 per cent in country towns such as Gloucester and Durham, which also drew visiting gentlemen to assizes, sessions and other business, their wives to shops, and both to a round of pleasure.

People of independent means were most numerous in the resorts. The contrast between resorts and typical market towns, may be seen in the case of the spa of Tunbridge Wells in 1841. The resort had 8,302 people, of whom 539 were leisured, including unmarried women and widowed gentlewomen, retired soldiers, professionals and businessmen, and one or two noblemen. In contrast, neighbouring Tonbridge had sixty leisured people among 3,115 people [10:*219*].

The expenditure of leisured households was a boost to the local economy. They encouraged, led and took part in social activities. In Lincoln in 1742, for example, the county gentry meeting for the races led by the Duke of Ancaster, decided to erect a better assembly room by subscription [142:*64*]. The position was rather different in France. A recent book on this period by Ruggiu compares the life of the genteel in Chester and Canterbury with that in Abbeville and Alençon, where noble and other elite residents contributed greatly to office-holding, but socially segregated themselves as far as clubs and cultural activities were concerned [143].

The middle orders or classes: education and training, religion, and living and working conditions

Socially, on personal business and in public duties, leisured people mixed with the more prosperous middle orders; from the 1780s the latter regarded themselves, and were regarded as, middle classes, though greatly divided by income and status [68:*70*]. The middle orders as a whole probably comprised between 17 and 25 per cent of the population, with a higher proportion in London and county centres than in many Midland and Northern manufacturing towns. The percentage increased everywhere by the early nineteenth century as the national income grew faster than the population and the prosperity of the middle orders increased more than that of the poorer majority. According to D'Cruze and other historians, the middle orders, unlike the lower, owned stock-in-trade or professional tools, and had liquid capital or mortgages, considerable household goods and often sizeable houses and even local fields. They performed public duties through office-holding on parish vestries or corporations; were executors of wills or trustees; churchwardens or chapel stewards; and later served on improvement commissions. The middle orders paid local poor rates and made donations and subscribed to hospitals and charity schools. [144:*181–6*; 122:*288–9*].

Between 1650 and 1750 the largely town-based professions developed in various ways, encouraged by, among other influences, the growing prosperity of the upper and middle orders, and made necessary by their specialist knowledge. To Anglican clergy were added Nonconformist ministers, especially after the Toleration Act of 1689. According to G. Holmes not only barristers but also attorneys and solicitors became increasingly respectable and busy. There were more and better-trained physicians and apothecaries with more useful drugs and instruments. Among the newer professions was government service, which became a secure career for civil servants, especially as their number swelled on account of the financial and administrative demands of the wars from 1689. Professional architects and surveyors, and journalists, writers and musicians all became established in London and to a lesser extent in provincial towns. School teachers, more numerous as instructors in the charity schools and private academies concentrating on modern subjects, were added, in the early eighteenth century, to schoolmasters in the grammar schools [145:*19–34 passim*].

After 1750 'the age of the lawyers' continued as the number and duties of attorneys increased, and the training of doctors continued to improve, partly because the new hospitals for the poor provided better facilities [146;147]. With other professionals, such as architects and engineers, they developed societies both for self-regulation and to support their interests. Taking one of the professions as an example, engineers were 'civil' and 'military' in the later eighteenth century, and by 1850 there were mechanical, electrical and mining engineers. With pioneers such as John Smeaton and I. K. Brunel adding to their status, the Institute of Civil Engineers opened in 1818 and the Institution of Mechanical Engineers in 1847. Anglican clergy grew more prosperous as the value of tithes increased, and their social status consequently increased. Both Anglican and Free Church ministers became more numerous as towns expanded and greater religious enthusiasm took hold from the 1790s. The civil service expanded, becoming more professional and better paid. While the incomes of teachers were less, many were being trained in the early nineteenth century. A handful of lawyers, judges and consultant doctors in London became wealthy. Although Holmes and Corfield disagree about whether the main impetus in the growth of the professions came between 1680 and 1730 or between 1750 and around 1800, there is a continuous development over the two centuries [148:*181–2 passim*].

The growing wealth, status and numbers of merchants, bankers and manufacturers were also a feature of this long period. In London from the 1670s, private bankers were making fortunes, and London merchants founded the Bank of England in 1694 to help finance the government and conduct private business. Among the wealthiest and most notable Londoners were Samson Gideon, a Portuguese Jew who made a fortune out of dealing with government stocks and trading company shares in the 1720s and 1730s, and then raised large government loans in the subsequent decades to fight the French; the West India merchant William Beckford, twice Lord Mayor; and brewers such as Samuel Whitbread in the late eighteenth century [149:*33–5, 53–5*].

The growth of provincial trade and industry created rivals to London's notable men. Newcastle and Gateshead produced William Cotesworth, coal owner, salt manufacturer and trader, who imported tropical goods in the decades around 1700 [150]. The wealthiest Liverpool West India and East India merchant at the beginning of the nineteenth century was probably John Gladstone [151].

From the beginning the middle orders had a small wealthy elite which stood apart from the mass of shopkeepers, master craftsmen and professionals. R. J. Morris has distinguished two or three status groups in the county centre, manufacturing town and regional metropolis by the early nineteenth century. For example, the Leeds middle class comprised three sections. First were the major manufacturers, merchants, bankers and other professionals, patrons of charities and other leaders; second were the shopkeepers, less prosperous professionals and manufacturers, who were important in chapels and neighbourhood communities; third were white-collar workers, clerks and teachers [122:*289–93*].

Throughout the period the identity of the middle class strengthened as its interests and ideology developed, and it became increasingly class-conscious. Its separation from the aristocracy and landed gentry – the upper classes – and from the lower classes became more obvious. Education and training, religious changes and living and working conditions all encouraged this process.

Many hundreds of mostly urban free grammar schools had been founded before 1650 to teach local boys Latin and Greek, and a few passed on to the Universities or Inns of Court and later became landed gentry, clergy, teachers or barristers. Numerous grammar schools opened in the following period, and many began to accept fee-paying boarders. These schools taught modern subjects such as mathematics and English, and perhaps history and geography, with book-keeping for those boys intended for trade. Non-classical and commercial subjects were taught by a growing number of fee-paying academies set up by individual teachers, many of whom were dissenters, with one or two assistants. Warrington Academy is perhaps the most well-known of these, and Derby had at least eight between 1770 and 1789. By the early nineteenth century a few grammar schools had become public schools and catered for fewer sons of tradespeople. Many of the other grammar schools expanded, as before, with a mixed curriculum. Private schools multiplied, some of them teaching painting, music, dancing and languages for girls as well as boys, in addition to modern and commercial subjects.

The Inns of Court continued to train barristers. Universities in London and Durham opened in the 1830s. Medical colleges appeared at Birmingham and Sheffield in 1828 and Leeds in 1831 so that intending physicians no longer needed to go to Scotland or Holland. Theological colleges opened, and the expanding towns absorbed a growing number of their graduates. For most tradesmen, craftsmen and professionals vocational training by apprenticeship remained typical, although the number of apprentices began to lag behind population growth. Apprenticeship meant living in the household of the master for seven years. Boys trained for relatively lucrative occupations, which depended on high premiums, came from middle-class or sometimes gentry homes. In London between 1715 and 1718 the average premium was £28, with many over £100 for attorneys and surgeons. Twenty years later those setting up shop in London were estimated to need a minimum of £20–£100 and a maximum of £5,000–£10,000. In the early nineteenth century training became more organised and formal. For example, Oxford and Cambridge graduates and fellows sat examinations, elementary teachers trained, and apothecaries were licensed and examined from 1815. Large premiums and start-up capital, and the expense of long college training all depended on a well-to-do background. Elevation from poor origins was almost impossible. The sources show families following a profession or trade for two or three generations, with sometimes a younger member engaged in other work. In eighteenth-century Colchester a father and son ran a charity school for decades, and a family named Shillito moved from the declining bay-making industry into the drinks trade. Families were often linked by business associations and common public duties, religion, friendship and even marriage. The self-confidence of the professions by the early nineteenth century may be seen in the formation of societies such as the Royal College of Surgeons in 1800 and the Institute of Civil Engineers in 1818, and the growth of provincial societies of attorneys from the 1730s and especially the 1800s. This self-confidence was based on growing numbers, higher earnings and more sophisticated work [152:65–8; 153:62; 70:54–9; 148:187].

Religion also helped to make the middle orders distinctive. While for the poorer majority indifference and little room in church discouraged attendance in many towns, during the eighteenth and early nineteenth centuries the more prosperous treated church-going as routine and even as a social occasion, owning or renting pews in prominent parts of the building where the sermon could be easily heard. Dissenting congregations originating in the seventeenth century, including the Presbyterians, Congregationalists and Quakers, were also dominated by pew-holding merchants, manufacturers and professionals who led the more numerous tradesmen and craftsmen. By 1800 religious fervour was emerging among sections of the middle classes, so that the Evangelicals among the Anglicans encouraged not only punctilious church-going but also prayers and bible-reading at home, and charitable works. Enthusiasm also affected the older Nonconformist congregations, which often founded new chapels after disputes over doctrine. While the Methodists drew more support from the lower orders, their meetings were mostly led by educated tradesmen and craftsmen.

The special family and living conditions of the middle orders also deserve discussion. Although the typical craft business relied on outworkers' production and on shop assistants, clerks and employees in attached workshops who were in the premises during the day, most heads of households were helped by wives, adult children and apprentices, who combined household and occupational work. Davidoff and Hall describe cases of middle-class business households in Birmingham and in East Anglian towns between around 1780 and 1850. Richard Tapper Cadbury was the son of a Devon Quaker serge-maker who had been apprenticed to a Gloucester draper and then worked for linen drapers in the City. He moved to Birmingham in 1794, married Elizabeth Head of Ipswich in 1796 and bought a sizeable house with a shop in the town centre. Gradually they built up a flourishing business. Although they had ten children, Elizabeth oversaw the business when Richard was away, checking orders and seeing callers. The daughters helped when necessary. The sons were apprenticed elsewhere: Benjamin ran the business from 1829 and John, with his father's financial help, became a tea and coffee merchant next door in 1824. While Richard took on public duties, presumably his retirement with a 'modest competency' gave him much leisure time [153:52–7].

Although help from family and servants was characteristic of middle-order society throughout the period, by the early nineteenth century growing prosperity was bringing changes to more affluent households. Daughters were more likely to have been to school or had tutors, and their greater education in basic modern subjects and the arts encouraged an interest in reading and cultured entertainment. As men grew wealthy, they hired more staff and were able to dispense with their wives' help. Families moved to the suburbs, away from the dirt and bustle of the town centre. By the 1790s Manchester had middle-class suburbs, and forty years later horse bus services enabled merchants and even their staff to live on the edge of the town. John Cadbury and his wife Candia lived in the centre of Birmingham between 1832 and 1834, and then moved to the suburb of Edgbaston. As a result, Candia was occupied with her children and the garden, and she and her children were cut off from direct contact with the business in Bull Street and the factory supervised by her husband. The typical separation of home and work place, which was to become common by the end of the century, had begun to appear [78:*30*; 153:*57*].

6

The elite and middle orders: entertainment, social relations and public duties

Recreations and other interests

Improved education, more leisure time and by 1800 greater religious zeal in some families, as well as increased wealth, encouraged recreational and social pursuits. Shrewsbury's entertainments before 1760 have been analysed in detail by McInnes; they included weekly assemblies, formal balls, racing, bowling, tennis, concerts and plays; facilities included coffee houses, public walks and bookshops. Shrewsbury's analysis has led to a discussion of how far leisure facilities existed in other towns [154:*66–70*; 155:*190*].

Reading became more widespread. While newspapers appeared in London in the later seventeenth century, 130 were launched in fifty-five provincial towns between 1701 and 1760. The well-to-do bought or read them in coffee houses, libraries and booksellers' premises. Although at first national news dominated provincial newspapers, more and detailed local information appeared later. Local printers published the papers; there were printers and booksellers in 212 towns by 1775. Booksellers, librarians and book clubs encouraged adult novel reading; children's books appeared around this time; poetry became popular and religious tracts were widely read by the 1790s.

Public concerts were supplemented by music societies and local choirs. Visiting drama companies performed plays of various types at increasingly sophisticated venues so that by 1805 there were 274 theatres. Assemblies provided opportunities for dancing and card-playing, and opportunities to see many friends and relations in one evening [6:*126–41*]. Travelling lecturers talked on various topics.

As P. Clark has written, there were innumerable clubs and societies. Some were for conversation, dining, drinking and gambling. In addition to music and book clubs, among the more intellectual were debating, scientific, artistic and botanical societies. The famous Royal Society began in 1662 and the Lunar Society in Birmingham in 1766. Freemasonry emerged in the early eighteenth century to pursue social and charitable purposes; by 1750 London had around 100 lodges and the provincial towns around sixty. County societies met in London to dine, raise money for charity and talk about county business. In Norwich in the 1730s 'the gentlemen and the better sort of tradesmen [kept] their clubs constantly every night'. The number of attendees varied from twelve to several hundred, with young adults well-represented. Meetings were frequent (if not nightly or weekly) and held at an inn. Although these meetings were subject to rules, they were sometimes noisy [156:*2–22*].

Sports, such as cockfighting and bull-baiting, entertained men until the late eighteenth century, when the middle classes became increasingly squeamish about these pursuits and treated them as a threat to public order [157:*77–9*]. Racing and shooting, and later boxing and cricket, were also popular. There was an increasing tendency for the fashionable to segregate themselves from the mass of the population in leisure activities [158:*247–9*].

Entertainment was particularly varied and well-organised at the resorts. Bath's Master of Ceremonies, Richard Nash, in the early eighteenth century drew up a code of behaviour for the entertainments. Visitors and residents at Tunbridge Wells in the 1840s were able to enjoy horseracing on the common, concerts, plays, the Hydropathic Establishment, and shampooing and vapour baths. The importance of the leisured classes for the economy of the spas and seaside towns is evident in the exceptional number of servants and suppliers of quality clothing such as dressmakers and milliners, and the range of luxury goods, some of which were displayed at leisure functions [10:*318–19*].

With the more rapid expansion of the urban middle classes from the 1780s, voluntary societies grew. Although a few national societies already existed in the early eighteenth century, including the Society for the Propagation of Christian Knowledge, which fostered the foundation of charity schools, countrywide associations became more numerous. The Nonconformist Royal Lancastrian Association and the Anglican National Society for the Education of the Poor encouraged schooling for working-class children from 1810 and 1811 respectively. According to Shoemaker, at least from the 1690s local societies began copying each other. For example, there were at least twenty Societies for the Reformation of Manners, which existed to effect prosecutions for vice in London, and others in up to forty provincial towns [159:*99–120*]. By 1800 voluntary societies were plentiful, including local groups for catching and prosecuting criminals, Societies for the Suppression of Beggars and numerous mechanics institutes following the foundation of the London Institution in 1824. Apart from the various cultural societies, there were religious associations to spread the Bible and simple tracts among the poor, charitable groups for voluntary poor relief in periods of high prices and heavy unemployment, and from the 1830s temperance societies to suppress drunkenness. These helped draw the middle classes together in common interests, usually under the leadership of the wealthiest citizens, but without too much individual commitment. They worked at a time when state intervention was minimal [160:*338–66*]. Morris, in a long and thorough study of Leeds voluntary societies, perhaps overemphasises their influence at a time when party and religious loyalties were divisive and growing [161:*chapters 7–12*].

The self-assertion of the middle orders gradually grew both in relation to the aristocracy and gentry and to the masses of the population. During the seventeenth century the more prosperous among the middle classes tried to emulate the landed elite in dress, behaviour and lavish spending. One of the attractions for the middle orders of visiting a spa was social activity, which enforced social mixing. Above all, the wealthiest townsmen joined the gentry by buying country estates. However, the wish of rich Londoners to buy land was declining in the early eighteenth century, according to N. Rogers. The development of the West End and more varied shops and entertainment made urban life more desirable; the growth of the National Debt and large trading companies offered alternative investments; and more landowners were living in London for the season or the whole year [162:*268–91*]. Although the middle orders in provincial towns continued to buy estates, by 1800 bigger communities with cultural and other attractions, and the availability of local business and urban property as investments, proved sufficient counter-attractions. Both in London and elsewhere, townspeople bought small neighbouring mansions and a few acres offering pleasant rural surroundings. By then the well-to-do in some towns had no contact with local gentry, except perhaps in the latter's roles as patrons of societies. Middle-class virtues of thrift, industry, business integrity and individualism were encouraged by the writings of Adam Smith and Jeremy Bentham and appeared to differentiate them from the upper and lower classes.

From the 1760s the middle orders displayed increasing political interest in London and in the major provincial towns such as Birmingham, Newcastle and Norwich. Money has shown that middle-class political consciousness in Birmingham led to an unexpected result in the Warwickshire parliamentary election of 1774, and finally resulted in the strength of the Birmingham Political Union in 1831 [163:*143, 158–243*]. After a long, intermittent struggle, townsmen won franchise reform from the landowners in 1832, and then supported the repeal of the Corn Laws in 1846. On the other hand the French Revolution, in addition to the huge increase in urban populations and periodic high food prices and unemployment, led to a permanent reaction by nearly all propertied people against the apparent threat from the lower classes, which in turn led to attempts at social control and spasmodic acts of repression. Calming and restraining disorderly or potentially disorderly workers was the partial motive for church-building in towns, the foundation of elementary schools, and the development of prison discipline. From the 1790s harsh legislation and occasional action by soldiers struck at agitation for parliamentary reform among working people. As the urban middle classes were also battling with the aristocracy and gentry, they were coming of age by 1850.

Town government and politics

Despite the great inequality in wealth and income, and difference in status among townspeople, numerous men played some part in urban government, the judicial process and elections. The mayor and aldermen or bailiffs, the sheriff (if one existed), the recorder and town clerk, and usually the councillors, treasurer (or chamberlain) and church-wardens of the parishes, came from the wealthiest 10 or 15 per cent of the inhabitants. These included tradespeople, professionals and gentry. Minor officials, usually elected annually, were often small retailers, craftsmen or artisans. They were also needed as parish overseers of the poor and more frequently as jurors. Typically, the freemen numbered from twelve to several thousand, with only limited regard for the town's size. Though a minority were non-resident, the rest were mostly householders in the various trades and crafts, including, by the early nineteenth century, many poorer inhabitants. Freedom came by apprenticeship and through birth or marriage. The alternatives for outsiders were purchase or gift by the corporation [164:99].

Towns differed widely in terms of local government and parliamentary representation. Eastwood shows that around 180 had municipal corporations, usually with a mayor, six to twelve aldermen and between around sixteen and thirty councillors. A few corporations, including Leeds, had narrow powers [165:58]. Municipal corporations were numerous in areas such as Devon and Cornwall, and few in others such as Derbyshire and Leicestershire, where the county town was the only borough. In around 75 per cent of the corporations councillors were co-opted for life by the existing members or just by the aldermen from among the freemen. Typically, aldermen were elected by and from among the councillors, and the mayor was elected annually from the aldermen or councillors. These 'close' corporations included Exeter, Bristol, Coventry, Leeds [164:*100*], Leicester [29:*67–9, 134*; 166], Liverpool [85:*71*], Lincoln [167:*174*], and High Wycombe [168:*115, 144*]. In the majority of the remaining corporations the freemen elected the chief officers and governing body. 'Open' corporations included that in Norwich [109:*26–7*].

The mayor and aldermen or former mayors were magistrates, who held petty and quarter sessions trying less serious crimes. The power to hold quarter sessions enabled many corporations to exclude county justices from their jurisdiction. While most of the officials (in effect, servants of the corporation) including constables, aletasters, leather searchers and town criers, were appointed annually and paid, the town clerk (an attorney) gave the administration permanency and earned fees, while the recorder, who was also a justice, gave the council legal advice. The jurors were not only needed at sessions but also at the borough court of record, which tried suits for debt, the court of pie powder and that of the clerk of the market. The corporation often owned the manor, with courts baron held every few weeks to record changes of property ownership, and courts leet, held twice yearly, which dealt with street nuisances, for example.

Although the City of London was much more populous than provincial towns, the Corporation was similar. The ratepayers in the Court of Wardmote annually elected around 210 common councillors and nominated twenty-six aldermen for life. Around 8,000 richer members of the ninety liveries or guilds in Common Hall helped elect the lord mayor and sheriffs. Thus the system was fairly democratic [170:*569–92*; 149:*chapter 9*].

Most corporations in 1650 had been created by charter during the middle ages, and especially in the previous century, either through the changes introduced locally by the Reformation or the wish of neighbouring gentry to secure election to Parliament through the town. Corporations gave the borough the right of permanent succession and a seal, and the right to own property, to sue in national courts and to make by-laws. If a corporation owned the market it had control over it; if it was a port it might have admiralty jurisdiction; and if it was on a river it might have conservancy powers. New charters affecting aldermen and councillors were granted by the Crown, especially in the 1680s.

Corporation income everywhere came from the ownership of property and lands. Often the corporation's estate was one of the largest in the town, though it made up only a small part of all urban property. Funds also came from the purchase of freedoms and fines on those refusing office. If the corporation owned the market and fairs, quays and the manor, their tolls and dues made a substantial contribution.

In the seventeenth century trades were normally grouped in guilds so that in some boroughs there was one for each trade and in others only one or two for all the major occupations. In Winchester from the 1660s there was a guild for the carpenters, joiners and masons; one for the tailors and hosiers; one for the butchers; and another for leather-using craftsmen [11:*176*]. Membership, which came through apprenticeship, inheritance or purchase, gave the right to practise a trade or craft, to control the quality of goods, and to participate in social activities. In around 25 per cent of the corporations, town freedoms were based on guild membership [170:*296–7*]. By 1700 provincial town guilds were in decline, with only occasional attempts to prosecute working non-members, so that annual dinners became the only function. In London, as Kellett has written, the guilds found controlling trades and crafts in the ever-growing suburbs an endless struggle, especially when their powers were weakened by common law decisions. However, an Act of 1712 and further legislation from 1750 enabled them to continue checks on freedoms, apprenticeship and the type and quality of goods. The crafts and retail trades were not legally thrown open until the 1830s [171:*381–9*].

A total of 156 municipal corporations had parliamentary representation. Voters were the freemen in ninety-one boroughs, whose numbers were often increased to swing the result, in the other boroughs electors were either particular property-owners, or ratepayers and residents, or corporation members [172:*89–90*].

Members were sometimes leading townsmen, and often local gentry or their nominees, who had the income and leisure for a part-time political career at Westminster. A seat in Parliament gave the member the chance to pursue his own interests and the interests of of the borough he represented. Election involved bribery, the extent of which depended on the number of voters.

Changes up to 1835 included the slow decline of the mayor, aldermen and councillors, and of the special corporation courts in nearly all boroughs, compared with the growing authority of the borough justices. London, Liverpool and Bristol were among the exceptions. The common councils were damaged, up to the 1720s, by religious and political factionalism, the exclusion of Nonconformists and opponents of the dominant political group, and the absorption of poor and highway matters by parish vestries and their officials; and from the mid-eighteenth century by the appointment in one town after another of statutory improvement commissioners to watch, light, pave and scavenge through the levying of rates. Many councils merely leased their property, appointed the officials annually and admitted freemen. Freedom became less significant, apart from at elections, as the supervision of crafts and trades and prohibition of non-freemen from shop-keeping came to an end. Meanwhile borough sessions work expanded in line with that of county quarter sessions, whose power often ended at borough borders.

The Webbs followed municipal corporation investigators in the early 1830s in condemning most of them as squabbling and corrupt, not only in the handling of parliamentary elections but also in the granting of leases on favourable terms and contracts to themselves and their friends, and lavish entertainment. More recent research has accepted the venality and faction-fighting to a great extent while emphasising other, more favourable, aspects of municipal government such as urban improvements and good intentions largely frustrated by lack of funds. Woodstock corporation decided in 1715 that common councillors should be admitted free to cockfights, and in 1759 that meadows should be let by a lottery among them [173:*216*]. Leicester corporation was justly accused in the 1820s of scandalous jobbing over gaol-building and the administration of charities [29:*145*]. On the other hand Exeter, (according to R. Newton), moved its markets to better sites between 1769 and 1783 and banned slaughtering within the walls, while spending profusely on feasts with wine supplied (at a price) by aldermen [174:*23*]. Hull 'close' corporation also tried to improve its streets and some of its buildings [58:*310–16*].

Corporation life was full of ceremony, political and constitutional disputes and related disorder. Colourful processions and rituals accompanied the election of the mayor at Michaelmas and bonfires and fireworks accompanied national anniversaries. To some extent all this reflected civic pride, also seen in the writing of town histories, celebrating and defending urban public life. A total of 129 town histories were written between 1780 and 1820 [175:*198–223*; 165:*63*; 176:*passim*]. Local patriotism was often deep rooted, as at Great Yarmouth between the Restoration and the 1720s [177:*32–3*].

Differences of religious opinion, and from the 1680s differences of parliamentary political opinion and over the governing charter, underlay local rows [178:*passim*]. There were frequent disagreements between aldermen and councillors, or between the council and freemen, or even within the council, on constitutional and political issues. Clubs and societies organised voters for civic elections. From the late seventeenth century until 1746 London's corporation was split between the Common Council, supporting the interests of the freemen, and the Court of Aldermen, which was trying to dominate the City's affairs [164:*107–8*; 149:*chapter 8*]. According to J. A. Phillips, in 1747, 1764, 1766 and 1767 the freemen of Maidstone stopped the corporation's attempts to end their voting power, the last three times by court action. The freemen were then divided at municipal elections into corporation and anti-corporation factions [179:*327–51*]. Liverpool's corporation in 1790–91 fought off the demands of the freemen for the replacement of the right of co-option of council members by election from the Common Council that is, themselves [85:*71*]. Occasionally, disputes stopped the appointment of a mayor or a council meeting, as at Walsall in the late seventeenth century [34:*52–82*].

From the 1680s the opposing parties in general elections were often called Whigs and Tories. Boroughs often divided on religious dissent, and on national issues such as Wilkes and the Middlesex Election or the abolition of the slave trade, though these were almost forgotten when local problems were considered. For example, Sweet has shown that in Chester in 1784 concern over the influence of the aristocratic Grosvenor family, which refused to support the citizens' scheme for a local canal and withheld hospitality, took precedence over the national debate about the Fox–North coalition and the East India Bill [172:*100*].

According to H. T. Dickinson's survey, out of 203 parliamentary boroughs, in around twenty the MPs were nominated through the purchase of the votes of the handful of electors; in forty-six boroughs one or two landlords owned the properties to which the franchise was tied; and in thirty-eight the corporation members controlled the voting. Around 50 per cent of the borough seats were partly or fully independent. Their electors, during the eighteenth century, numbered between several hundred and 8,000–12,000, the largest being Westminster. Thirty-three of them had more than a thousand voters, often a large minority of the adult males. These were the borough constituencies most often canvassed and contested, with the electors displaying considerable freedom of opinion [164:*17–22*].

In addition to the 180 municipal corporations, there were more than 100 manorial boroughs that were subject to a lord with real or nominal authority; although they did not have their own sessions jurisdiction, they had mayors or bailiffs, and aldermen and councillors, as well as the courts found in corporations. Little Arundel in Sussex, Wisbech in Cambridgeshire, Altrincham in Cheshire, and Alnwick in Northumberland, as well as the populous Westminster were manorial boroughs [180:*17*; 170:*127–211*]. While most manorial boroughs were located in small towns, they included by 1750 two of the largest, Birmingham and Manchester.

The majority of around 400 or 450 towns were governed by a manorial court and parish vestry, with specific duties sometimes being handled by property trustees. Sheffield had Town Trustees and twelve Capital Burgesses to pay for clergy, church, bridge and road repairs, and charities. The court baron of the manor registered property conveyances, tried suits of small debts and controlled open fields and commons. The court leet checked urban nuisances such as roaming pigs or street encroachments, and dealt with market offences such as selling with improper weights or selling poor-quality goods, as at Ormskirk in Lancashire, according to Duggan [21:*6–16*]. Dues, fees and fines paid for all these tasks. The vestry dealt with Poor Law and highway business, appointing the necessary overseers and surveyors, and levying rates. In Manchester the court leet appointed an increasing number of officials (138 by 1756), and its wide role made it the most important authority in the eighteenth century. In contrast, in Birmingham the court leet's power was either always weaker or declined much earlier [170:*99–112*; 85:*104–6*; 49:*97*].

The reforms introduced by Whig governments in the 1830s included sweeping parliamentary and municipal changes. The 1832 Reform Act reduced the parliamentary representation of the smaller boroughs in favour of the more populous counties. Instead of 202 English boroughs returning 403 MPs, 168 boroughs were responsible for 324. Fifty-six boroughs lost both MPs and thirty lost a single MP. Twenty-two new two-member and nineteen single-member seats were created, chiefly in the new industrial areas. Influence on elections, which had actually been growing since 1800, was reduced but not ended. Although existing electors kept their franchise for life, the vote was extended to £10 householders. In the long run, this made the electors more solidly middle class and disenfranchised poor freemen in large electorates. An inquiry into municipal corporations in 1833 found much amiss, and the 1835 Act replaced 178 corporations with councils elected by ratepayers, and indirectly-chosen mayors and aldermen, both with narrower powers. Rights, privileges and duties were abolished. Birmingham and Manchester became corporations in 1838, followed by Bolton, Sheffield, Salford, Bradford, Warrington and Wakefield in the 1840s. Prosperous tradesmen and professional people became councillors, a third in south-east Lancashire being textile masters.

There had been almost no English constitutional change for more than a century. There had been no new charters to alter the structure and powers of municipal corporations, and borough parliamentary representation had hardly altered. From the 1770s radicals in some towns had been trying to change municipal constitutions through new by-laws, with only occasional success. Parliamentary reformers had also been pressing unsuccessfully for representational change. Suddenly, in the 1830s the reform of Parliament and municipal government, for all its limitations, set a crucial precedent for future constitutional changes.

7

The lower orders

Work, food and poor relief

More than 60 per cent of the urban population was made up of wage-earners. Their incomes enabled most families to subsist, except in years of bad harvest or trade depression, when many turned to public or private poor relief and were threatened by malnutrition. Wives and older children earned low wages and families took in lodgers to make survival possible. Unlike the middle classes, the lower orders had no property, few household goods and sometimes no wares for sale or tools for work; and they did not hold public office. Throughout the period most workers, including textile workers, shoemakers and garment makers, handled materials at home. Many others, for example, in the metal trades, were employed in workshops attached to a manufacturer's or craftsman's home. Works housing tens of employees, such as breweries or, later, machine shops, grew and factories with several hundred men, women and children were numerous by 1800. The increasing number of shops (especially selling food, drink, and clothing) and street traders employed a huge number. Building work as a labourer or journeyman craftsman was important everywhere and especially in growing towns. Transport also absorbed labour, so that the large ports were full of workers on wharves and mariners' families. In inland towns innkeepers and carriers needed assistance.

Food and drink took up more than 60 per cent of the income of such families. Bread and beer were the staples for much of the period, with white bread spreading from South to North in the eighteenth century. By 1800 potato consumption was spreading in the north-west and often adulterated tea drinking was becoming common. The consumption of meat, especially bacon, varied according to income, and sugar was still a luxury in the early nineteenth century. Food was monotonous and usually sparse, according to Feinstein's survey, although the variety and quality of food probably improved slightly between 1750 and 1850 [80:*106*].

Rent, fuel (coal in towns), clothing and boots absorbed the rest of the meagre earnings, apart from the income the male householder spent with his friends at the local alehouse.

Until almost the end of the eighteenth century poor relief went mainly to widows and orphans, and the sick and old. From the mid-1790s unemployment among the able-bodied was more serious as labour grew too plentiful, especially in years of depression marked by high food prices and low industrial production. Some types of work declined permanently, including cotton handloom weaving and East London silkweaving in the 1830s and 1840s. Charitable societies, corporation members, and well-to-do people collected money for food and coal or provided work in winter. Parish poor relief generated from rates was more important, and outdoor relief continued alongside the workhouse. Industrialists in the North used the Poor Law as 'an unemployment insurance system', as Boyer wrote; when workers were laid off, they collected outdoor relief, and were re-employed when they were needed as demand for their output returned [181:*233–4*].

The occupations and abodes of paupers in the 1830s and 1840s are known in detail through research by D. R. Green, A. G. Parton and S. Alexander. In Birmingham in 1847 paupers were concentrated in close courts in the eastern part. They included artisans in the metal trades, hucksters and unskilled workers such as washerwomen and seamstresses. Women outnumbered men by two to one. In St Giles' parish in London, where precarious unskilled work predominated among the inhabitants of dark, ill-ventilated and undrained tenements, the occupations of those applying for relief between 1832 and 1862 are known. The men were labourers and employees of manufacturers, and also those who worked in street trading, building and service; the women were in service, manufacturing, charring and hawking, with some prostitutes. Less skilled, lower-paid manufacturing was over-represented; restrictions on the range of female employment meant that the occupations of these women were almost the same as for those who did not need relief [182:*47–9,69–70*; 183].

In contrast, a minority of workers, such as some metal craftsmen and cotton machine spinners, earned above-average wages and there is growing evidence of saving from the late eighteenth century. Under the auspices of pubs and beerhouses, which existed in nearly every street, sick and burial clubs and groups for buying goods such as clothes or watches, flourished, for example those of the Black Country. A small amount of social insurance came to 600,000 friendly society members by 1800, and after 1816 artisans were legally encouraged to use savings banks. These workers were also able to afford a fuller and more varied diet, and perhaps to rent dwellings of four or five rooms in better streets. They were the 'aristocracy of labour'.

Schooling, beliefs and amusements

The beliefs and ideas of the lower orders are difficult to gauge. Magic and folklore held sway among most artisans and labourers for the early part of the period. Charms and rituals with the use of herbs and roots were used by most people to cure illness. Although doctors were never seen or wanted by most people, quacks and patent medicines were increasingly used when earnings allowed, as well as opium by the early nineteenth century and alcohol to suppress pain. Astrologers were consulted for advice, on medical problems, decision-making and future prospects [69:*31–5*; 184:*113–17*].

Such a superstitious outlook existed alongside the absence of universal primary education, and religious apathy. Scholars have disagreed about the precise timing and extent of the spread of literacy. Literacy, measured by the ability to sign one's name, increased from just under 50 to 56 per cent for men across England between 1700 and 1775, aided by the new charity schools; with the absence of sufficient new schools and burgeoning population growth, it then fell in the large towns, only increasing again with the opening of more government-funded schools from the 1830s; official figures in 1851 showed 69.3 per cent male and 54.8 per cent female literacy. However, 50 per cent or more of the male lower orders were unable to write for most of the period. Although a higher proportion read, probably hesitantly, the cost of reading materials and lack of practice made working-class communication entirely oral in practice [185:*9–23*].

Church attendance by poor people in towns was weak throughout. Religious apathy was probably encouraged by dull and lengthy church sermons, Sunday fatigue among some workers, and insufficient church space. Insufficient Anglican churches were built in the growing towns during the eighteenth century and between 1800 and 1820. Although building picked up with government and wealthy private support for free seating, it was still far from adequate. The spread of bibles and religious tracts in the early nineteenth century was too small to have much effect.

While the revival of Nonconformist denominations from the 1790s gained some working-class support in towns, especially among the Baptists, Methodism made a bigger contribution. Wesley had concentrated his preaching in towns in which the Anglican clergy were failing, and by the religious census of 1851, Methodism was strong in the industrial towns of Lancashire, Yorkshire, Staffordshire and Cornwall, drawing the working classes to chapel and training a few as leaders by allowing them to act as stewards. In the large towns it made the greatest contribution to lower-class worship, though only a small minority of the total can have been affected.

The religious institution the workers used most extensively was the Sunday School. Begun in the 1780s and run by local committees of clergy and laity, Sunday-School teaching spread everywhere, with the textile towns at the heart of the movement. Partly intended as a contribution to social order by occupying young people, Sunday Schools taught reading and writing with basic religious instruction. The movement touched a huge number of working people, with up to 75 per cent of their children attending in 1851, though historians disagree about its permanent effect [185:*13–15,110*; 186:*13*].

But on the whole there was little elementary culture to stir the minds of the masses. It is therefore not surprising that their entertainments were rough and visual. According to H. Cunningham and J. Rule large numbers gathered at fairs to see plays, puppet-shows and working models; menageries with gorgeously-uniformed bandsmen, as well as lions and elephants, and various exotic stalls; horse races; and later at prize fights and circuses. Dog and cock-fighting were popular, despite efforts to suppress them in the early nineteenth century. Finally the basic alehouse diversions of dice, cards, shove-penny and similar games were sources of entertainment for men in the evenings [187:*35–8,79*; 188: *19,22–3,33–4*].

For a minority of artisans and labouring people, conversion to Methodism in the early nineteenth century stopped drinking and attendance at cruel sporting events. Magic held sway in the countryside, where the elements were crucial and people knew each other, rather than in the anonymity of large towns, where new ideas spread freely. During the eighteenth century at least better-paid manual workers followed middle-class families in slowly abandoning medical magic, instead taking the advice of apothecaries when they bought medicines. While not many could be admitted to the few and small new hospitals, more attended the dispensaries which were also springing up in the larger towns. By 1850 life was improving in various ways for many lower-class townspeople.

Crime and violence

Poverty and periodic unemployment in proximity to apparent affluence were the basis of crime and violence. Various types of theft were the most common crimes, including burglary. Opportunities and motives were strong in London and the large provincial towns, with their many wealthy houses, shops laden with attractive goods and well-dressed people, and the sheer need of many poor people in rookeries where hiding from constables or policemen was easy. In London, professional criminals such as forgers, receivers of stolen goods and constantly-active pickpockets were relatively few, and most thefts were acts of occasional impulse when opportunity, hardship or attraction were great. Most perpetrators were not caught, and a sizeable proportion of the lower orders stole at some time. Crime was particularly severe during bursts of unemployment, and after a war demobilised soldiers caused it to rise. Although the temptation to steal was strong among the poorest, many more skilled people such as apprentices or former apprentices were among those hung at Tyburn [188: *226–44*; 189:*1–16,300*].

Individual cases of assault were numerous before the middle of the eighteenth century. Group acts of violence were endemic, taking place in towns rather than in the country, except in the case of the Swing Riots of 1830, because farmworkers were dispersed and usually controlled by magistrates. Urban growth encouraged mob activity. Shoemaker has shown that disturbances occurred almost daily in London in the early eighteenth century because of huge numbers, overcrowding and the absence of an adequate police force. Motives were varied, but sexual immorality, illicit trading practices, and religious and political issues were no doubt significant in many instances. These involved a few dozen men and women (or more) of varying social background, with the initiative coming sometimes from the political elite, sometimes from ordinary crowd members [190:*188–222*]. Some of the most damaging to property included riots in 1736, which were provoked by government restrictions on gin sales and the fact that building workers and weavers were losing work to Irish labourers, leading to an East End mob destroying Irish public houses. Strong anti-Roman Catholic feeling and hatred of conspicuous wealth seem to have dominated the Gordon Riots of 1780, which lasted three days and involved the destruction of Catholic churches and houses and attacks on public buildings. On the other hand, food riots were relatively rare in London because supply was quite sound.

Until the end of the century disturbances in times of dearth to stop the movement of grain, cheese or meat and enforce a 'just' price were extensive at the site of markets, inns and warehouses, and at the homes of middlemen. Food riots occurred at seaports to stop exports in the early eighteenth century, and in the growing Northern textile towns in the 1780s. Industrial workers concerned about wages rioted in London in 1766–9 and much of the manufacturing North and Midlands in 1842. Local outbreaks of machine-breaking occurred throughout the eighteenth century and it became much more general in 1811–16, when the Luddites attacked machines in the Nottinghamshire and Leicestershire hosiery districts and in the textile areas of the West Riding and

Lancashire, to stop wage cuts. Lancashire power looms were again smashed in 1826. Politically-motivated riots struck London in 1768 over John Wilkes' election to Parliament as Member for Middlesex, and in 1816 as a result of radical meetings at Spa Field. Radicalism emerged in the rapidly growing provincial towns from the 1790s, and when the movement for parliamentary reform reached a crisis in October 1831 there were disturbances in Derby and Nottingham, and prolonged rioting in Bristol. Although the Chartists spoke of violence, and some were implicated in the industrial troubles in 1842, they were not responsible for these outbreaks. Finally, Birmingham had the 'Church and King' riots against the Nonconformists in 1791, the most bitter religious demonstration after London's Gordon Riots.

Disorderly behaviour declined in the 1830s and 1840s as first London, then provincial towns, had disciplined policemen. Together with the new railways, which allowed the swift movement of the army, they ended the Chartist threat. Riots have greatly interested recent historians, who have shown that many typical mob members were skilled artisans, and have debated how far revolutionary impulses overlay the basic industrial motives of the Luddites [188:*196–225*; 69:*109–37*; 191].

Riots were the occasional product of crowd meetings. Civic ceremonies, visits by royalty or noblemen and popular activities drew almost everybody onto the streets in the seventeenth and eighteenth centuries. By the end of the eighteenth century crowds were sometimes huge for celebrations, elections, speeches or executions. M. Harrison counted at least 245 crowd events in Bristol between 1790 and 1835, and the radical Henry Hunt's visit to Manchester in 1831 attracted more than 30 per cent of the population [158:*228–37*; 192:*4,112–19*].

The rise of working clubs and unions

Class identity among the lower orders and their sense of social separation from the rest of society grew in the late eighteenth century. Three historians have written that the working class emerged between about 1790 and 1840, E. P. Thompson pointing to the period 1790–1832, H. J. Perkin dating it between 1815 and

1820, and John Foster attributing it to the 1830s. These ideas aroused much debate among historians, as Morris has shown. It is safe to suggest that the working class emerged slowly from the 1760s in London, and elsewhere between about 1780 and 1850, with periodic bursts of organised social and political activity in 1768 in London, and in the early 1790s, 1815–20, 1830–3, 1842 and 1848. Growing co-operation between working people may be seen in benefit clubs, trades unions and political organisations. The working class consisted not just of the factory proletariat (as Marx thought) but also of outworking craftsmen, domestic workers, miners and farm labourers, yet its social and political manifestations were mainly urban, and tended to exclude the deferential, dependent domestic servants and very poor [193: 7–12].

During the eighteenth century workers' combinations were widespread among craftsmen. Though most members worked in their own homes, or alone, or in tiny groups outdoors, they were encouraged by close contact in towns and through the growth of workshops and later of factories. Local clubs federated into wider organisations such as the hatters' union, and strikes over wages, hours or the use of blackleg labour were common. Despite the Combination Acts (1800–24) urban unions with better organisation, such as London printers, tailors, shoemakers and ship-builders, expanded after 1800, while unions in industrial areas found conditions harder. Further growth was notable until 1850 among newer or more skilled manufacturers such as cotton-spinners, engineers and shipwrights, with only a few per cent of working people being members. Prothero and R. Church have shown that several outstanding leaders emerged from among the artisans, including shipwright John Gast of London, the idealist John Doherty of Manchester and bobbin netmaker Gravenor Henson of Nottingham [47:*320*; 194: *passim*]. Attempts to form district and national unions were made in the 1820s and 1830s, for example among carpenters in 1827 and spinners in 1829–30. Co-operative societies based on the ideas of Robert Owen were temporarily founded in many towns in the early 1830s, and there were equitable labour exchanges in London and Birmingham. In the early 1830s social organisations peaked in the short-lived Grand National Consolidated Trades Union of 1834 which aimed to combine all workers, and which was strongest among shoe-makers and tailors in London [188:*201–13*; 195:*162–4*; 196].

Following artisan support for parliamentary reform in London in the wake of the Wilkes episode in 1768, political radicalism appeared nationally in the early 1790s under the immediate inspiration of the French Revolution. Urban clubs with some artisan members, meetings with greater support and the sale of hundreds of thousands of Tom Paine's *Rights of Man* (1791–2) were principal features. Radical agitation was great in 1816–19, with clubs, meetings, demonstrations and petitions stimulated by a radical press read by urban-based working men, and revived in 1830–1, when it was marked by huge rallies and unions in London and the manufacturing towns. Later, Chartism was by far the century's biggest working-class movement for radical parlia-mentary reform, with cheap newspapers, rallies, conventions and petitions to Parliament in 1839, 1842 and 1848. Beginning in London and Birmingham, the impetus spread to Northern towns, deriving support more from outworkers than factory workers and especially from within the textile trades. High food prices and unemployment largely created and underpinned Chartism as they had earlier political agitations. At the same time there was opposi-tion to the new Poor Law, often from the same men, its organisa-tion derived from the Ten Hour movement for improved factory conditions in 1833, and working-class anti-Corn Law societies in industrial towns, which were led and supported by employers. These developments of combinations and political activities from the eighteenth century to the 1840s have been outlined in several general studies [195:*66–7,182–6,206–7*; 197: *chapters 1–5*; 69:*73–6*; 198:*1–146*].

The degree of class consciousness among working people has been debated. One view suggests that the political movements of the different social groups encouraged class feeling, and that social class and comment about it dominated life, with Foreign Secretary Lord Palmerston referring to 'every class in society' in 1850. A contrary view stresses divisions among workers. Artisans lived in different streets and had their own pubs, societies and entertain-ments, despising poorer unskilled labourers. The various agita-tions were at least partly the work of different groups, reflecting the contrast in earnings, skill and industrial structure and pointing to the relative absence of common feelings of deprivation and exploitation. Although class consciousness may have been inspired temporarily in some places by special situations, town workers remained disunited in outlook and by varying degrees of economic security in the early nineteenth century. As Gadian has shown for Lancashire cotton towns and Koditschek in detail for Bradford, class consciousness and class conflict were greater in towns dominated by factory manufacture, still involving only a small proportion of working people. However, there was an enormous growth of social and political activity consisting of benefit and radical clubs, trades unions, radical leaders and newspapers, meetings and demonstrations which helped to widen the experience of the majority of the urban workers [69:*71–7*; 195:*167–73*; 199:*256–7*; 200].

Conclusion

Urban England was transformed between 1650 and 1850. While towns were just islands in a rural sea in the seventeenth century, in 1851 more than 50 per cent of the people lived in them. Though London's economy changed, the capital continued to dominate, with its huge population growth. The leading provincial towns in 1850 had risen from a tiny size largely because of the expansion of industry and trade, and towns dependent on leisure and defence had appeared. Part of the wealth towns created built houses – now mostly brick – and smaller sums created public buildings, factories, docks and urban amenities. National income growth in excess of population increase almost exclusively boosted the living standards of the upper and middle orders, bringing them, in turn, social and political advantages. The wage-earning majority of manual workers benefited much less.

The foundations were laid for the creation of an urban nation in the late nineteenth century. Almost 80 per cent of the population lived in towns in 1901. The years between 1850 and 1900 were marked by unprecedented absolute population growth, the huge expansion and improvement of the physical structure, and rising working-class living standards as real wages grew; and diet, housing and public health, working conditions and leisure activities improved with the further development of urban class identities.

Appendices

Appendix I. *The population of some larger towns between 1650 and 1800*

London	1650: c.375,000	1750:	c.650,000
Norwich	1650: c.20,000		
	1693: 28,881	1752:	36,196
Bristol	1650: c.15,000	—	
	1695: 19,403	—	
Exeter	1671–2: 13,500		
Newcastle	1665: 12,000		
York	1670: 10,000–10,900	c.1730:	10,800
		c.1770:	12,800
Yarmouth	1670: c.10,000	—	
Colchester	1670: c.9,000	1750:	c.8,000
Oxford	1667: c.9,000	—	
Worcester	1670: c.8,000–9,000	1782:	13,104
Cambridge	1674: c.8,500	1728:	7,778
Ipswich	1689: 8,308	—	
Canterbury	1676: 7,431	—	
Chester	1664: c.7,000	1720:	c.10,000
		1774:	14,713
Leeds	1700: c.7,000	1750:	c.10,000
		1771:	16,380
Salisbury	1695: 6,976	—	
Coventry	1694: 6,714	1748:	12,117
Deptford	1676: 6,625	—	

Shrewsbury	1672: 6,000–6,500	1750:	8,141
Plymouth	1700: 6,000	1750:	13,000–14,000
Bury St Edmunds	1675: 5,500–6,100	—	
Nottingham	1676: 5,500	1739:	10,010
		1779:	17,771
Hull	1673: c.5,800		
Tiverton	1705: 5,000–6,000	1750:	c.4,500 [?]
Manchester and Salford	1660: c.5,000	1717:	10,000–12,000
Reading	1660: c.5,000		
Chatham	1700: c.5,000	1750:	c.6,000
Gloucester	1695: 4,756	1743:	5,291
Leicester	1670: 4,600	1730:	c.8,000
Northampton	1675: c.4,500	1746:	5,136
Kings Lynn	1676: 4,500		
Birmingham	1676: 4,400	1750:	23,688
		1770:	30,804
Hereford	—	1775:	5,592
Carlisle	1676: 3,863		
	1688: 4,301		
Sunderland	—	1719:	c.6,000
Portsmouth	1664: 3,500	1750:	c.10,000
	1676: 4,300		
Sheffield	1700: under 3,500	1736:	9,695
		1757:	12,001
Warrington	—	1780:	9,501
Whitehaven	1693: 2,222	1713:	4,000
		1762:	9,062
Liverpool	1673: c.1,500	1750:	22,000
	1700: 5,714	1774:	34,407
Wolverhampton	—	1750:	7,454
Bath	1660: c.1,100	1742:	6,000–6,500

Source: 5: *3–25*; 15: *129–183*; C. M. Law, 'Some Notes on the Urban Population of England and Wales in the eighteenth century', *Local Historian* 10 (1972–3).

Appendix II. *The largest towns, 1801 and 1851*
(Towns with more than 50,000 people in 1851)

Town	1801	1851
London	1,088,000	2,491,000
Liverpool	88,358	375,955
Manchester	75,000	367,955
Birmingham	69,384	232,841 (with Aston)
Bristol	68,088	137,328
Plymouth	43,532	103,092
Norwich	36,832	68,195
Sheffield	35,344	103,626
Bath	34,160	54,000
Portsmouth	33,226	72,126
Leeds	30,669	101,343
Hull	29,516	95,389
Nottingham	28,861	58,419
Newcastle	28,294	89,156
Sunderland	c.24,500	70,576
Leicester	16,953	60,642
Stockport	14,850	54,000
Preston	11,887	68,537
Brighton	7,339	65,569
Bradford	6,393	52,501

The total for Bradford in 1851 covers the built-up area only, and that for Nottingham in 1801 excludes people living in housing beyond the open fields.

Appendix III. *Other Towns, 1801 and 1851*

Town	1801	1851
Exeter	17,398	32,823
York	16,846	36,303
Coventry	16,049	36,811
Chester	15,052	27,766
Yarmouth	14,845	26,880
Shrewsbury	14,739	23,104
Wolverhampton	12,565	49,985
Bolton	12,549	39,923
Oxford	11,921	27,843
Colchester	11,520	19,443
Worcester	11,352	27,677
Ipswich	10,880	32,759
Derby	10,832	40,609
Whitehaven	10,628	35,614
Chatham	10,505	21,886
Kings Lynn	10,096	20,530
Cambridge	10,087	27,815
Reading	9,770	22,175
Carlisle	9,521	26,310
Canterbury	9,356	14,100
Gloucester	7,718	17,572
Salisbury	7,668	9,455
Bury St Edmunds	7,655	13,900
Hereford	6,828	12,108

Bibliography

The history of English towns in the 250 years before the present study begins is discussed in another book in this series, by A. Dyer, *Decline and Growth in English Towns, 1400–1640* (London 1991). Four books cover English urban history in the sixteenth and seventeenth centuries: P. Clark and P. Slack, eds., *Crisis and Order in English Towns, 1500–1700* (London 1972); P. Clark and P. Slack, eds., *English Towns in Transition, 1500–1700* (London 1976); J. Patten, *English Towns, 1500–1700* (Folkestone 1978); and S. B. Jack, *Towns in Tudor and Stuart Britain* (Basingstoke and London 1996).

For the early part of the period, A. McInnes, *The English Town, 1660–1760* (London 1980) provides a short general survey. R. Sweet, *The English Town, 1680–1840: Government, Society and Culture* (Harlow 1999), has an administrative and political approach, without overlooking society and culture.

For a wide range of information on individual towns, see the *Victoria Histories of the Counties of England*. The more useful volumes are those written from the 1950s. See also the *Urban History of Britain*, Vol. II: *1540–1840* (Cambridge 2000).

Many more specialised books and papers, often relating to a single town or theme, had to be excluded from this list.

1. A. L. Beier and R. Finlay, 'Introduction: the Significance of the Metropolis', in Beier and Finlay, eds., *London 1500–1700: The Making of the Metropolis* (Harlow 1986) is a collection of essays on an important subject.
2. P. Corfield, 'Urban Development in England and Wales in the Sixteenth and Seventeenth Centuries', in D. C. Coleman and

A. H. John, eds., *Trade, Government and Economy in Pre-industrial England* (London 1976).

3. R. Davis, *English Overseas Trade, 1500–1700* (Basingstoke 1973) is a short survey.

4. A. L. Beier, 'Engine of Manufacture: the Trades of London', in Beier and Finlay, eds., *London 1500–1700*.

5. C. W. Chalklin, *The Provincial Towns of Georgian England: a Study of the Building Process, 1740–1820* (London 1974), while mainly concerned with the financial aspects of house building in seven towns, has two chapters on provincial urban economic development. For the population figures for individual towns, see P. Clark, K. Gaskin and A. Wilson, *Population Estimates of English Small Towns, 1550–1851* (Leicester 1989), and P. Clark and J. Hosking, *Population Estimates of English Small Towns, 1550–1851* (Leicester 1993). Settlements with fewer than 500 people were 'marginal' towns, and there were probably about 600 towns of more than 500 people. Population estimates mostly relate to parishes, which often included a rural hinterland, and the number is approximate.

6. P. Clark, 'Small Towns in England, 1550–1850' and M. Reed, 'The Cultural Role of Small Towns in England 1600–1800', in P. Clark, ed., *Small Towns in Early Modern Europe* (Cambridge 1995), a group of essays with much new material.

7. J. Godber, *History of Bedfordshire* (Bedford 1969), is a long survey that is partly relevant to this study.

8. H. T. Graf, 'Leicestershire Small Towns and Pre-industrial Urbanisation', *Leicestershire Archaeological and Historical Society Transactions LXVIII* (1994), pp. 98–117.

9. J. B. Rogers, 'The Market Area of Preston in the Sixteenth and Seventeenth Centuries', *Geographical Studies* III, i (1956), pp. 49–55. This is an original approach by a scholar writing in the 1950s.

10. C. W. Chalklin, 'The Towns', in A. Armstrong, ed., *The Economy of Kent, 1640–1914* (Woodbridge 1995) concerns a highly urbanised part of England. Chelmsford, the county town in Essex, has been studied in H. Grieve, *The Sleepers and the Shadows. Chelmsford: a Town, its People and its Past*, Vol. 2, *From Market Town to Chartered Borough, 1608–1888* (Chelmsford 1994).

11. A. Rosen, 'Winchester in Transition, 1580–1700', in P. Clark, ed., *Country Towns in Pre-industrial England* (Leicester 1981).

12. W. B. Stephens, *Seventeenth Century Exeter* (Exeter 1958) writes with special reference to trade.

13. N. R. Goose, 'Decay and Regeneration in Seventeenth-century Reading: a Study in a Changing Economy', *Southern History* 6 (1984), pp. 53–74.

14. M. Reed, 'Economic Structure and Change in Seventeenth Century Ipswich', in Clark, ed., *Country Towns*.

15. P. Corfield, *The Impact of English Towns, 1700–1800* (Oxford 1982) is a comprehensive survey with an emphasis on larger towns.

16. E. A. Wrigley, 'A Simple Model of London's Importance in Changing English Society and Economy, 1640–1750', *Past and Present* 37 (1967) is an influential paper.

17. R. Porter, *London: A Social History* (London 1994) is a readable survey that includes much relevant material.

18. P. Borsay, *The English Urban Renaissance: Culture and Society in the Provincial Town, 1660–1770* (Oxford 1989) is a perceptive study of cultural improvement. On the street scene, with more polite behaviour and the control of nuisances, see P. J. Corfield, 'Walking the City Streets: the Urban Odyssey in Eighteenth Century England', *Journal of Urban History* 16 (1990), pp. 133–57.

19. L. Weatherill, *Consumer Behaviour and Material Culture in Britain, 1660–1760* (London 1988) includes material about household contents.

20. C. B. Estabrook, *Urbane and Rustic England: Cultural Ties and Social Spheres in the Provinces, 1660–1780* (Manchester 1998).

21. M. Duggan, *Ormskirk: the Making of a Modern Town* (Stroud 1998).

22. W. E. Minchinton, 'Bristol: Metropolis of the West in the Eighteenth Century', in P. Clark, ed., *The Early Modern Town: a Reader* (London 1976). The book includes reprints of essays on London, Norwich, Leeds and Sheffield which are relevant to the period 1650–1800.

23. F. E. Hyde, *Liverpool and the Mersey: an Economic History of a Port, 1700–1970* (Newton Abbot 1971).

24. J. E. Williams, 'Whitehaven in the Eighteenth Century', *Economic History Review*, 2nd series, VIII (1956), pp. 393–402.

25. J. Stobart, 'An Eighteenth-century Revolution? Urban Growth in North-west England, 1664–1801', *Urban History* 23 (1996) part I, pp. 26–47.

26. W. G. Hoskins, *Industry, Trade and People in Exeter, 1688–1800* (Manchester 1935) discusses the history of the town against the background of the changing fortunes of serge manufacturing.

27. J. D. Chambers, 'Population Change in a Provincial Town: Nottingham, 1700–1800', in L. S. Pressnell, ed., *Studies in the Industrial Revolution* (London 1960), pp. 103, 122.

28. A. Henstock and M. Bennett, 'Part II: Early Modern Nottingham', in J. Beckett, ed., *A Centenary History of Nottingham* (Manchester 1997).

29. J. Simmons, *Leicester Past and Present* Vol. I: *Ancient Borough to 1860* (London 1974).

30.   R. G. Wilson, *Gentlemen Merchants: the Merchant Community in Leeds, 1700–1800* (Manchester 1971).
31.   A. P. Wadsworth and J. de L. Mann, *The Cotton Trade in Industrial Lancashire, 1600–1780* (Manchester 1931), is still valuable.
32.   P. Corfield, 'A Provincial Capital in the Late Seventeenth Century: the Case of Norwich', in P. Clark and P. Slack, eds., *Crisis and Order in English Towns, 1500–1700* (London 1972).
33.   C. Gill, *History of Birmingham: Manor and Borough to 1865* (London 1952), partly relates to this period.
34.   E. J. Homeshaw, *The Corporation of the Borough and Foreign of Walsall* (Walsall 1960) is partly relevant; see also M. Rowlands, *Masters and Men in the West Midland Metalware Trades before the Industrial Revolution* (Manchester 1975).
35.   D. Hey, *The Fiery Blades of Hallamshire: Sheffield and its Neighbourhood, 1660–1740* (Leicester 1991) is a substantial study of a relatively short period.
36.   R. Davis, *The Rise of the English Shipping Industry* (London 1962).
37.   E. A. Wrigley, 'Urban Growth and Agricultural Change: England and the Continent in the Early Modern Period', in P. Borsay, ed., *The Eighteenth Century Town, 1688–1820* (London 1990) is a collection of previously published papers which includes some critical comment. Wrigley discusses general issues of the relationship between large and small European towns, and between town and country, in 'City and Country in the Past: a Sharp Divide or a Continuum?', *Historical Research* LXIX (1991), especially pp. 109–16. He also considers the slower growth of continental towns in *People, Cities and Wealth: the Transformation of Traditional Society* (Oxford 1987), pp. 177, 179ff.
38.   F. Sheppard, *London, 1808–1870: the Infernal Wen* (London 1971).
39.   Hoh-cheung and Lorna H. Mui, *Shops and Shopkeeping in Eighteenth Century England* (London 1989).
40.   N. McKendrick, J. Brewer and J. H. Plumb, *The Birth of a Consumer Society: the Commercialisation of Eighteenth Century England* (London 1982).
41.   L. S. Pressnell, *Country Banking in the Industrial Revolution* (Oxford 1956) is the standard work.
42.   A. Everitt, 'The English Urban Inn, 1560–1760', in A. Everitt, ed., *Perspectives in English Urban History* (London 1973) includes a discussion on this century.
43.   A. Everitt, 'Country, County and Town: Patterns of Regional Evolution in England', in Borsay, ed., *Eighteenth Century Town*.
44.   M. Noble, 'Growth and Development in a Regional Urban System: the Country Towns of Eastern Yorkshire, 1700–1850', *Urban History Yearbook* (1987), pp. 1–21.

45. A. F. J. Brown, *Essex at Work, 1700–1815* (Chelmsford 1969) includes information on towns.
46. E. Gillett, *A History of Grimsby* (London 1970) is partly relevant to this study.
47. R. A. Church, *Economic and Social Change in a Midland Town: Victorian Nottingham, 1815–1900* (London 1966).
48. C. S. Davies, *A History of Macclesfield* (Manchester 1961, includes relevant sections; see also G. Malmgreen, *Silk Town: Industry and Culture in Macclesfield 1750–1835* (Hull 1985).
49. E. Hopkins, *The Rise of The Manufacturing Town: Birmingham and the Industrial Revolution* (Stroud 1998) considers both the economy and society of this leading town between around 1750 and 1840.
50. J. Prest, *The Industrial Revolution in Coventry* (Oxford 1969).
51. T. C. Barker and J. R. Harris, *A Merseyside Town in the Industrial Revolution: St Helens, 1750–1900* (London 1959), links industrialisation with urban growth.
52. R. S. Neale, *Bath: A Social History, 1680–1850* (London 1981) is the standard history of the spa in its golden age.
53. P. Hembry, *The English Spa, 1560–1815: a Social History* (London 1990) is a comparative survey.
54. G. Hart, *A History of Cheltenham* (Leicester 1965), includes information on this period.
55. J. Whyman, *Aspects of Holidaymaking and Resort Development within the Isle of Thanet, with Particular Reference to Margate, c. 1736 to c. 1840* (New York 1981); see also J. K. Walton, *The English Seaside Resort: A Social History 1750–1914* (Leicester 1983).
56. E. W. Gilbert, *Brighton: Old Ocean's Bauble* (London 1954) is a survey of Brighton's history, of which the first part is relevant.
57. P. McGrath, ed., *Bristol in the Eighteenth Century* (Newton Abbot 1972) includes an essay on trade by W. E. Minchinton; for trade and the economy to 1850, see also K. Morgan, 'The Economic Development of Bristol, 1700–1850', in M. Dresser and P. Ollerenshaw, eds., *The Making of Modern Bristol* (Tiverton 1996), pp. 48–75.
58. G. Jackson, *Hull in the Eighteenth Century: a Study in Economic and Social History* (London 1972).
59. A. T. Patterson, *A History of Southampton, 1700–1914*, Vol. I (Southampton 1966).
60. F. M. L. Thompson, 'Town and City', in Thompson, ed., *The Cambridge Social History of Britain*, Vol. I: *Regions and Communities* (Cambridge 1990) draws on C. M. Law, 'The Growth of Urban Population in England and Wales, 1801–1911', *Transactions of the Institute of British Geographers* 41 (1967), pp. 125–45.
61. E. A. Wrigley, 'Break or Accelerator? Urban Growth and Popula-

tion Growth Before the Industrial Revolution', in Ad van der Woude, Akira Hamayi and Jan de Vries, eds., *Urbanization in History: a Process of Dynamic Interaction* (Oxford 1990).

62. D. Souden, 'Migrants and the Population Structure of Later Seventeenth Century Provincial Cities and Market Towns', in P. Clark, ed., *The Transformation of English Provincial Towns, 1600–1800* (London 1984).

63. J. G. Williamson, *Coping with City Growth during the British Industrial Revolution* (Cambridge 1990).

64. A. Sharlin, 'Natural Decrease in Early Modern Cities: a Reconsideration', *Past and Present* 79 (1978) is based on continental cities as well as London and other English towns.

65. M. Anderson, *Family Structure in Nineteenth-century Lancashire* (London 1971), analyses especially Preston in 1851.

66. M. D. George, *London Life in the Eighteenth Century* (London 1926) is a classic social history of the period.

67. J. Landers, *Death and the Metropolis: Studies in the Demographic History of London, 1670–1830* (Cambridge 1993).

68. E. Gauldie, *Cruel Habitations* (London 1975) is a history of nineteenth-century working-class housing.

69. J. Walvin, *English Urban Life, 1776–1851* (London 1984) is a useful survey.

70. L. D. Schwarz, *London Life in the Age of Industrialisation: Entrepreneurs, Labour Force and Living Conditions, 1700–1850* (Cambridge 1992) is based like note 71 below, on primary sources.

71. P. Earle, *The Making of the English Middle Class: Business, Society and Family Life in London, 1660–1730* (London 1989).

72. A. F. J. Dulley, 'People and Homes in the Medway Towns: 1687–1783', *Archaeologia Cantiana* LXXVII (1962), pp. 160–76.

73. R. Grassby, 'The Personal Wealth of the Business Community in Seventeenth-century England', *Economic History Review*, 2nd series, XXIII (1970), pp. 220–34.

74. For incomes around 1760 see P. Mathias, 'The Social Structure in the Eighteenth Century: A calculation by Joseph Massie', *Economic History Review*, 2nd series (1957–8), pp. 42–3.

75. P. H. Lindert and J. G. Williamson, 'English Workers' Living Standards during the Industrial Revolution: a New Look', *Economic History Review*, 2nd series (1983), pp. 1–25.

76. D. Woodward, *Men at Work: Labourers and Building Craftsmen in the Towns of Northern England, 1450–1750* (Cambridge 1995).

77. J. K. Walton, *Lancashire: A Social History, 1558–1939* (Manchester 1987).

78. R. Scola, *Feeding the Victorian City: The Food Supply of Manchester, 1770–1870* (Manchester 1992).

79. N. F. R. Crafts, *British Economic Growth During the Industrial Revolution* (Oxford 1985) discusses living standards within the wider perspective of economic growth.

80. C. H. Feinstein, 'Pessimism Perpetuated: Real Wages and the Standard of Living in Britain During and After the Industrial Revolution', *Journal of Economic History* 58 (1998), pp. 625–52 is the most recent study on this controversial subject.

81. P. Borsay, 'The Development of Provincial Urban Culture, c. 1680–1760', in Borsay, ed., *The Eighteenth Century Town*; for the occupational structure of a major port, Newcastle between 1660 and 1720, see J. M. Ellis, 'A Dynamic Society: Social Relations in Newcastle-upon-Tyne 1660–1760', in P. Clark, ed. *The Transformation of English Provincial Towns, 1600–1800* (London 1984), pp. 217–20.

82. D. R. Green, *From Artisans to Paupers: Economic Change and Poverty in London, 1790–1870* (Aldershot 1995). The long decline in economic and social life between the crisis of 1825–26 and the mid-1840s is a central theme of the book.

83. W. A. Armstrong, *Stability and Change in an English County Town: a Social Study of York, 1801–51* (London 1974) draws particularly on the census returns of 1841 and 1851 cf. note 65 above.

84. P. Taylor, *Popular Politics in Early Industrial England: Bolton, 1825–1850* (Keele 1995); for the occupational structure of a leading port, Bristol in 1841, see P. Ollerenshaw and P. Wardley, 'Economic Growth and the Business Community in Bristol since 1840', in Dresser and Ollerenshaw, eds., *The Making of Modern Bristol*.

85. F. Vigier, *Change and Apathy: Liverpool and Manchester during the Industrial Revolution* (Cambridge, MA 1970).

86. W. G. Rimmer, 'Working Men's Cottages in Leeds, 1770–1840', in *Thoresby Society Publications* XLVI, part 2 (1961), pp. 165–99.

87. J. Langton, 'Residential Patterns in Pre-Industrial Cities: Some Case Studies from Seventeenth-century Britain', in J. Barry, ed., *The Tudor and Stuart Town, 1530–1688* (Harlow 1990).

88. R. J. Dennis, *English Industrial Cities of the Nineteenth Century: a Social Geography* (Cambridge 1984).

89. John D. Wirth and Robert L. Jones, *Manchester and Sao Paulo: Problems of Rapid Urban Growth* (Stanford, CA 1978) is a comparison of Manchester with a Brazilian city.

90. J. Patten, *English Towns, 1500–1700* (Folkestone 1978).

91. E. L. Jones, 'The Reduction of Fire Damage in Southern England, 1650–1850', *Post-medieval Archaeology* 2 (1968), pp. 140–9.

92. M. W. Beresford, *East End, West End: the Face of Leeds during Urbanisation, 1684–1842* (Publications of the Thoresby Society LX

and LXI for 1985 and 1986) is the detailed history of building in a major town.

93. E. Chadwick, *Report on the Sanitary Condition of the Labouring Population of Great Britain, 1842*, M. W. Flinn, ed. (Edinburgh 1965), is a well-known contemporary source.

94. S. D. Chapman, 'Working-Class Housing in Nottingham during the Industrial Revolution', in Chapman, ed., *The History of Working-Class Housing: a Symposium* (Newton Abbot 1971).

95. C. W. Chalklin, 'Estate Development and the Beginnings of Modern Tunbridge Wells, 1800–40', *Archaeologia Cantiana* C (1985), pp. 285–98.

96. Essays by R. Newton on Exeter and T. H. Lloyd on Leamington Spa, in M. A. Simpson and T. H. Lloyd, eds., *Middle Class Housing in Britain* (Newton Abbot 1977).

97. K. Hudson, *Building Materials* (London 1972), is a short survey.

98. C. G. Powell, *An Economic History of the British Building Industry, 1815–1979* (London 1980) contains two chapters relevant to this book.

99. T. Bannister, 'The First Iron-framed Buildings', *The Architectural Review* (1950), pp. 231–46.

100. J. M. Crook and M. H. Port, *The History of the King's Works*, Vol. VI *1782–1851* (London 1973).

101. A. Satoh, *Building in Britain: the Origins of a Modern Industry* (Aldershot 1995). The relevant earlier part is a new introduction to the subject.

102. L. Clarke, *Building Capitalism: Historical Change and the Labour Process in the Production of the Built Environment* (London 1992) is a theoretical (Marxist) approach, useful apart from the fact that the role of attorneys is overlooked.

103. R. Rodger, *Housing in Urban Britain, 1790–1914* (Basingstoke 1989) summarises the conclusions of E. W. Cooney, 'The Building Industry', in R. Church, ed., *The Dynamics of Victorian Business* (London 1980), pp. 142–60 and R. Price, *Masters, Unions and Men: Work Control in Building and the Rise of Labour, 1830–1914* (Cambridge 1980), pp. 20–6.

104. S. Webb and B. Webb, *English Local Government: Statutory Authorities for Special Purposes* (London 1922).

105. J. Stovold, ed., *Minute Book of the Pavement Commissioners for Southampton, 1770–1789*, Southampton Record Series XXXI (1990), illustrates the work of a paving authority.

106. F. H. W. Sheppard, *Local Government in St Marylebone, 1688–1835* (London 1958).

107. M. C. Buer, *Health, Wealth and Population in the Early Days of the*

Industrial Revolution (London 1926) is interesting in spite of the revision of some of its conclusions by more recent research.

108. J. A. Hassan, 'The Impact and Development of Manchester's Water Supply, 1568–1882', *Transactions of the Historic Society of Lancashire and Cheshire for 1983* (1984), pp. 26–33, includes some information about the development of the supply of water in other English towns.

109. M. E. Falkus, 'The British Gas Industry before 1850', *Economic History Review*, 2nd series XX (1967), pp. 494–508.

110. E. P. Hennock, 'Urban Sanitary Reform a Generation before Chadwick?', *Economic History Review*, 2nd series X (1957), pp. 113–20, disputes the view of B. Keith Lucas, 'Some Influences affecting the Development of Sanitary Legislation', in *Economic History Review*, 2nd series VI (1953–54), pp. 291–9, that sanitary conditions improved.

111. T. F. Reddaway, *The Rebuilding of London after the Great Fire* (London 1940).

112. S. McIntyre, 'Bath: the Rise of a Leisure Town, 1660–1800', in P. Clark, ed., *Country Towns in Pre-industrial England.*

113. J. Summerson, *The Life and Work of John Nash, Architect* (London 1980). Some of the buildings appear to have been modelled on buildings in Paris; see pp. 140, 165, 167.

114. *Survey of London XXVII: Spitalfields and Mile End New Town* (1957); the *Survey* volumes are full of detail on the history of buildings in London.

115. *Dictionary of National Biography*: Sir Thomas Neale.

116. D. J. Olsen, *Town Planning in London: the Eighteenth and Nineteenth Centuries* (New Haven 1964) discusses the building of Bedford Square and adjoining streets on the Bedford Estate as an example of such covenants.

117. J. Summerson, *Georgian London* (London 1945, reprinted 1962) is a classic survey.

118. J. R. Ward, 'Speculative Building at Bristol and Clifton, 1783–1793', *Business History* XX (1978), pp. 3–18.

119. S. Blake, *Pittville, 1824–1860* (Cheltenham 1988) is a brief analysis of the surviving manuscripts.

120. M. I. Thomis, *The Town Labourer and the Industrial Revolution* (London 1974).

121. *Survey of London XXXII: St James Westminster* (1963) is an example.

122. R. J. Morris, 'The Middle Class and British Towns and Cities of the Industrial Revolution, 1780–1870', in D. Fraser and A. Sutcliffe, eds., *The Pursuit of Urban History* (London 1983).

123. S. D. Chapman and J. N. Bartlett, 'The Contribution of Building

Clubs . . . to Working-Class Housing in Birmingham', in Chapman, ed., *The History of Working-class Housing*.

124. M. W. Beresford, 'The Making of a Townscape: Richard Paley in the East End of Leeds, 1771–1803', in C. W. Chalklin and M. A. Havinden, eds., *Rural Change and Urban Growth 1500–1800* (London 1974) also includes essays on Bath, Cumbrian towns and new towns.

125. J. M. Baines, *Burton's St Leonards* (Hastings 1956) mentions that Burton bought a country estate at Tonbridge and built St Leonards.

126. H. Hobhouse, *Thomas Cubitt, Master Builder* (London 1971). Beginning as a journeyman carpenter, Cubitt became a millionaire, borrowing extensively to lend to smaller builders on his projects, and making money from the sale of improved ground rents, pp. xxiii, 341–3.

127. C. W. Chalklin, *English Counties and Public Building, 1650–1830* (London 1998).

128. K. Grady, *The Georgian Public Buildings of Leeds and the West Riding*, Thoresby Society Publications LXII for 1987 (Leeds 1989) contains all surviving information on building costs though it ignores price changes.

129. D. Swann, 'The Pace and Progress of Port Investment in England, 1660–1830', *Yorkshire Bulletin of Economic and Social Research* 12 no. 1 (1960), pp. 33–9, is a brief survey.

130. J. Longmore, 'Liverpool Corporation as Landowners and Dock Builders, 1709–1835', in C. W. Chalklin and J. R. Wordie, eds., *Town and Countryside: the English Landowner in the National Economy, 1660–1860* (London 1989).

131. S. D. Chapman, *The Cotton Industry in the Industrial Revolution* (London 1972).

132. J. Parry Lewis, *Building Cycles and Britain's Growth* (London 1965) begins in the early eighteenth century.

133. A. K. Cairncross and B. Weber, 'Fluctuations in Building in Great Britain, 1785–1849', in E. M. Carus Wilson, ed., *Essays in Economic History III* (London 1962).

134. H. A. Shannon, 'Bricks: a Trade Index, 1785–1849', in *ibid*.

135. T. S. Ashton, *Economic Fluctuations in England, 1700–1800* (Oxford 1959).

136. F. Sheppard, V. Belcher and P. Cottrell, 'The Middlesex and Yorkshire Deeds Registries and the Study of Building Fluctuations', *The London Journal* 5 (1979), pp. 176–217.

137. J. Burnett, *A Social History of Housing, 1815–1970* (London 1980). The first part is relevant.

138. J. H. Treble, 'Liverpool Working-class Housing, 1801–51' in S. D. Chapman, ed., *Working-class Housing*.

139. I. C. Taylor, 'The Court and Cellar Dwelling: The Eighteenth Century Origin of the Liverpool Slum', *Transactions of the Historic Society of Lancashire and Cheshire* CXXII (1970), pp. 71–86.

140. C. Feinstein, 'Capital Formation in Great Britain', *Cambridge Economic History of Europe* VII, part I (Cambridge 1978), pp. 28–96.

141. C. Morris, ed., *The Illustrated Journeys of Celia Fiennes, c. 1682–1712* (London 1984); contemporary short comments on towns are also to be found in D. Defoe, *A Tour through the Whole Island of Great Britain* (London 1724).

142 C. W. Chalklin, 'Capital Expenditure on Buildings for Cultural Purposes in Provincial England, 1730–1830', *Business History* XXII no. 1 (1980), pp. 51–70.

143. F. J. Ruggiu, *Les Elites et les Villes Moyennes en France et en Angleterre (XVIIe-XVIII siecles)* (Paris 1997).

144. S. D'Cruze, 'The Middling Sort in Eighteenth-Century Colchester: Independence, Social Relations and the Community Broker', in J. Barry and C. Brooks, eds., *The Middling Sort of People: Culture, Society and Politics in England, 1550–1800* (Basingstoke 1994); on the middle classes see also J. Seed, 'From "Middling Sort" to Middle Class in Late Eighteenth- and Early Nineteenth-century England', in M. L. Bush, ed., *Social Orders and Social Classes in Europe since 1500* (Harlow 1992) and M. Hunt, *The Middling Sort: Commerce, Gender and the Family in England* (Berkeley and Los Angeles 1996); for middle-class philanthropy in London see D. T. Andrew, *Philanthropy and Police: London Charity in the Eighteenth Century* (Princeton 1990).

145. G. Holmes, *Augustan England: Professions, State and Society 1680–1730* (London 1982).

146. R. Robson, *The Attorney in Eighteenth Century England* (London 1959).

147. M. E. Fissell, *Patients, Power and the Poor in Eighteenth Century Bristol* (Cambridge 1991).

148. P. J. Corfield, *Power and the Professions in Britain, 1700–1850* (London 1995).

149. G. Rudé, *Hanoverian London, 1714–1808* (London 1971).

150. J. M. Ellis, *A Study of the Business Fortunes of William Cotesworth, c. 1668–1726* (New York 1981).

151. S. G. Checkland, *The Gladstones: A Family Biography* (London 1971).

152. C. Brooks, 'Apprenticeship, Social Mobility and the Middling Sort, 1550–1800', in Barry and Brooks, eds., *The Middling Sort.*

153. L. Davidoff and C. Hall, *Family Fortunes: Men and Women of the English Middle Class, 1780–1850* (London 1987).

154. A. McInnes, 'The Emergence of a Leisure Town: Shrewsbury 1660–1760', *Past and Present* 120 (August 1988), pp. 53–84.

155. P. Borsay, 'Debate: The Emergence of a Leisure Town: or an Urban Renaissance?', *Past and Present* 126 (February 1990), pp. 190–200.

156. P. Clark, *Sociability and Urbanity: Clubs and Societies in the Eighteenth Century City* (Leicester 1986) is a short survey.

157. J. M. Golby and W. Purdue, *The Civilisation of the Crowd: Popular Culture in England, 1750–1900* (London 1984).

158. P. Borsay, 'All the Town's a Stage: Urban Ritual and Ceremony, 1660–1800', in P. Clark, ed., *Transformation of English Towns*.

159. R. B. Shoemaker, 'Reforming the City: the Reformation of Manners Campaign in London, 1690–1738', in L. Davison *et al.*, eds., *Stilling the Grumbling Hive: The Response to Social and Economic Problems in England, 1689–1750* (Stroud 1992). This is a collection of essays with an emphasis on London and Bristol.

160. R. J. Morris, 'Voluntary Societies and British Urban Elites, 1780–1850: An Analysis', in Borsay, ed., *The Eighteenth Century Town*.

161. R. J. Morris, *Class, Sect and Party: The Making of the British Middle Class. Leeds 1820–1850* (Manchester 1990).

162. N. Rogers, 'Money, Land and Lineage: The Big Bourgeoisie of Hanoverian London', in Borsay, ed., *The Eighteenth Century Town*.

163. J. Money, *Experience and Identity: Birmingham and the West Midlands, 1760–1800* (Manchester 1977).

164. H. T. Dickinson, *The Politics of the People in Eighteenth Century Britain* (Basingstoke 1994) is a survey with much information on corporations.

165. D. Eastwood, *Government and Community in the English Provinces, 1700–1870* (Basingstoke 1997) includes a chapter on towns.

166. R. W. Greaves, *The Corporation of Leicester, 1689–1836* (London 1979).

167. J. W. F. Hill, *Tudor and Stuart Lincoln* (Cambridge 1956); see also Hill, *Georgian Lincoln* (Cambridge 1966).

168. L. J. Ashford, *The History of High Wycombe from its Origins to 1880* (London 1980).

169. J. T. Evans, *Seventeenth-century Norwich: Politics, Religion and Government, 1620–1690* (Oxford 1979).

170. S. Webb and B. Webb, *The Manor and the Borough*, Part II (1908).

171. J. R. Kellett, 'The Breakdown of Gild and Corporation Controls over the Handicraft and Retail Trades in London', *Economic History Review*, 2nd series, 10 (1958), pp. 381–9.

172. R. Sweet, 'Freeman and Independence in English Borough Politics', *Past and Present* 161 (1998), pp. 89–90.

173. P. Langford, *Public Life and the Propertied Englishmen, 1689–1798* (Oxford 1991).

174. R. Newton, *Eighteenth Century Exeter* (Exeter 1984).

175. J. Barry, 'Provincial Town Culture, Urbane or Civic?', in J. H. Pittock and A. Wear, eds., *Interpretation and Cultural History* (Basingstoke 1991).

176. R. Sweet, *The Writing of Urban Histories in Eighteenth-century England* (Oxford 1997).

177. P. Gauci, *Politics and Society in Great Yarmouth, 1660–1722* (Oxford 1996).

178. P. Halliday, *Dismembering the Body Politic: Particular Politics in England's Towns, 1650–1730* (Cambridge 1998).

179. J. A. Phillips, 'From Municipal Matters to Parliamentary Principles: Eighteenth Century Borough Politics in Maidstone', *Journal of British Studies* 27 (1988), pp. 327–51.

180. M. Rowlands, 'Government and Governors in Four Manorial Boroughs in the West Midlands 1600–1700', *Journal of Regional and Local Studies* 13 (1993), pp. 1–19.

181. G. R. Boyer, *An Economic History of the English Poor Law 1750–1850* (Cambridge 1990).

182. D. R. Green and A. G. Parton, 'Slums and Slum Life in Victorian England: London and Birmingham at Mid-century', in S. M. Gaskell, ed., *Slums* (Leicester 1990).

183. S. Alexander, *Women's Work in Nineteenth-century London: a Study of the Years 1820–1850* (London 1983) is a specialised study; women servants in London are discussed by P. Seleski, 'Women, Work and Cultural Change in Eighteenth and Early Nineteenth Century London', in T. Harris, ed., *Popular Culture in England, c. 1500–1850* (London 1995), pp. 143–67.

184. B. Reay, 'Popular Religion', in B. Reay, ed., *Popular Culture in Seventeenth-century England* (London 1985); the essays on London and Bristol by P. Burke and J. Barry respectively are also relevant.

185. M. Sanderson, *Education, Economic Change and Society in England, 1780–1870* (Basingstoke 1983) provides a clear summary; for a study of literacy in the mid-nineteenth century see W. B. Stephens, *Education, Literacy and Society, 1830–70* (Manchester 1987).

186. W. R. Ward, *Religion and Society in England, 1790–1850* (New York 1972) is one of several studies of religious change in the period.

187. H. Cunningham, *Leisure in the Industrial Revolution* (London 1980). The first half of the book is relevant.

188. J. Rule, *Albion's People: English Society, 1714–1815* (Harlow 1992) is one of several recent social histories of the eighteenth and early nineteenth centuries.

189. F. McLynn, *Crime and Punishment in Eighteenth-century England*

(London 1989) is one of several books on crime in the period, partly in towns [Chapter 1 deals with London]. See also P. Linebaugh, *The London Hanged: Crime and Civil Society in the Eighteenth Century* (London 1992).

190. R. B. Shoemaker, 'The London "Mob" in the Early Eighteenth Century' in Borsay, ed. *The Eighteenth Century Town*, one of several studies of London disorder at the time; for political unrest in London in the 1670s and 1680s, see T. Harris, *London Crowds in the Reign of Charles II: Propaganda and Politics from the Restoration until the Exclusion Crisis* (Cambridge 1987).

191. J. Stevenson, *Popular Disturbances in England, 1700–1870* (London 1979) is the standard textbook.

192. M. Harrison, *Crowds and History: Mass Phenomenon in English Towns, 1790–1835* (Cambridge 1988).

193. R. Glen, *Urban Workers in the Early Industrial Revolution* (London 1984) especially discusses Stockport. The books by the three historians are E. P. Thompson, *The Making of the English Working Class* (London 1963), H. Perkin, *The Origins of Modern English Society, 1780–1880* (London 1969), and J. Foster, *Class Struggle and the Industrial Revolution* (London 1974), the last relating to Northampton, Oldham and South Shields. In a five-class model, R. S. Neale sees the working class (like the middle class) in two parts: *Class and Ideology in the Nineteenth Century* (London 1972). R. J. Morris, *Class and Class Consciousness in the Industrial Revolution 1780–1850* (London 1979) is a short general survey of the whole subject.

194. I. J. Prothero, *Artisans and Politics in Early Nineteenth-century London: John Gast and his Times* (Folkestone 1979).

195. E. J. Evans, *The Forging of the Modern State: Early Industrial Britain, 1783–1870* (Harlow 1983).

196. A. E. Musson, *British Trade Unions, 1800–1875* (Basingstoke 1972) is a short survey.

197. J. Belchem, *Popular Radicalism in Nineteenth-century Britain* (Basingstoke 1996).

198. A. Briggs, ed., *Chartist Studies* (London 1959), pp. 1–146, contains special studies of Manchester, Leeds and Leicester.

199. D. S. Gadian, 'Class Consciousness in Oldham and Other Northwest Industrial Towns, 1820–50', in R. J. Morris and R. Rodger, eds., *The Victorian City: a Reader in British Urban History, 1820–1914* (Harlow 1993).

200. T. Koditschek, *Class Formation and Urban Industrial Society: Bradford, 1750–1850* (Cambridge 1990).

Index

Abbeville, 48
Aberdeen, 33
academies (schools), 51
Acts of Parliament, see Statutes
aldermen, 59–65
alehouses, 67, 68, 70, 71, 74
Alençon, 48
Alexander, S., 67
almshouses, 41
Alnwick, 64
Altrincham, 64
America, trade with, 7, 15
American War of Independence, 13
Amsterdam, 10
Ancaster, Duke of, 48
Anderson, M., 17
Anglicans, 52, 57, 59, see also churches
apprenticeship, apprentices, 3, 17, 31,
    51, 53, 59, 61, 71
architects, 49
aristocrats, as landowners, 34–5, 51,
    57; see also London, aristocracy
    and gentry
Arundel, 64
Ashton, Lancashire, 25
Ashton, T. S., 45
assembly rooms, assemblies, 40, 48,
    55
asylums, pauper lunatic, 40, 42
attorneys, see lawyers

banking, banks, bankers, 5, 10, 11, 16,
    39, 50, 68, see also London, banks
    and bankers
baptisms, 18, 19
Barbon, Nicholas, 38
barracks, in towns, 9, 14, 41
Bath, building, 30, 34, 36
    occupations, 25–6

population, 78, 79
    spa, 8, 9, 14, 56
    working-class living standards, 22
Beckford, William, 50
Beier, A. L., 2
Bentham, Jeremy, 58
Beresford, M. W., 37, 38
Berlin, 9
Beverley, 11
Birmingham, 14, 15, 33, 51, 56, 73
    Bull Street, 54
    Cadbury business and family, 53–4
    government, 64, 65
    house-building, 30, 36, 37, 38
    metalware manufacturing, 8, 13
    pauper occupations, 67
    politics, 58, 74
    population, 78, 79
    riots, 72
birth rate, 17
Blackburn, 13
Black Country, 8, 13, 15, 68
Blake, S., 38
Blandford, 29
Bolton, 13, 20, 25, 65, 80
books, booksellers, book clubs, 2, 6, 23,
    55, 56
boroughs, municipal, 59–65
Borsay, P., 6, 23
Boston, 11
Boyer, G. R., 67
Bradford, 12, 65, 75, 79
bricklayers, 31, 37
bricks, 29–30, 31, 44–6
Brighton, 14, 79
Bristol, 14
    commerce, 4, 5, 7
    contact with countryside, 6, 16
    corporation, 59, 61

New Studies in Economic and Social History

Titles in the series available from Cambridge University Press

12. M. Collins, *Banks and Industrial Finance, 1800–1939*
    ISBN 0 521 55271 0 (hardback) 0 521 55782 8 (paperback)

13. A. Dyer, *Decline and Growth in English Towns, 1400–1640*
    ISBN 0 521 55272 9 (hardback) 0 521 55781 X (paperback)

14. R. B. Outhwaite *Dearth, Public Policy and Social Disturbance in England, 1550–1800*
    ISBN 0 521 55273 7 (hardback) 0 521 55780 1 (paperback)

15. M. Sanderson, *Education, Economic Change and Society in England*
    ISBN 0 521 55274 5 (hardback) 0 521 55779 8 (paperback)

16. R. D. Anderson, *Universities and Elites in Britain since 1800*
    ISBN 0 521 55275 3 (hardback) 0 521 55778 X (paperback)

17. C. Heywood, *The Development of the French Economy, 1700–1914*
    ISBN 0 521 55276 1 (hardback) 0 521 55777 1 (paperback)

18. R. A. Houston, *The Population History of Britain and Ireland, 1500–1750*
    ISBN 0 521 55277 X (hardback) 0 521 55776 3 (paperback)

19. A. J. Reid, *Social Classes and Social Relations in Britain, 1850–1914*
    ISBN 0 521 55278 8 (hardback) 0 521 55775 5 (paperback)

20. R. Woods, *The Population of Britain in the Nineteenth Century*
    ISBN 0 521 55279 6 (hardback) 0 521 55774 7 (paperback)

21. T. C. Barker, *The Rise and Rise of Road Transport, 1700–1990*
    ISBN 0 521 55280 X (hardback) 0 521 55773 9 (paperback)

22. J. Harrison, *The Spanish Economy*
    ISBN 0 521 55281 8 (hardback) 0 521 55772 0 (paperback)

23. C. Schmitz, *The Growth of Big Business in the United States and Western Europe, 1850–1939*
    ISBN 0 521 55282 6 (hardback) 0 521 55771 2 (paperback)

24. R. A. Church, *The Rise and Decline of the British Motor Industry*
    ISBN 0 521 55283 4 (hardback) 0 521 55770 4 (paperback)

25. P. Horn, *Children's Work and Welfare, 1780–1880*
    ISBN 0 521 55284 2 (hardback) 0 521 55769 0 (paperback)

26. R. Perren, *Agriculture in Depression, 1870–1940*
    ISBN 0 521 55285 0 (hardback) 0 521 55768 2 (paperback)

27. R. J. Overy, *The Nazi Economic Recovery, 1932–1939* (second edition)
    ISBN 0 521 55286 9 (hardback) 0 521 55767 4 (paperback)
28. S. Cherry, *Medical Services and the Hospitals in Britain, 1860–1939*
    ISBN 0 521 57126 X (hardback) 0 521 57784 5 (paperback)
29. D. Edgerton, *Science, Technology and the British Industrial 'Decline', 1870–1970*
    ISBN 0 521 57127 8 (hardback) 0 521 57778 0 (paperback)
30. C. A. Whatley, *The Industrial Revolution in Scotland*
    ISBN 0 521 57228 2 (hardback) 0 521 57643 1 (paperback)
31. H. E. Meller, *Towns, Plans and Society in Modern Britain*
    ISBN 0 521 57227 4 (hardback) 0 521 57644 X (paperback)
32. H. Hendrick, *Children, Childhood and English Society, 1880–1990*
    ISBN 0 521 57253 3 (hardback) 0 521 57624 5 (paperback)
33. N. Tranter, *Sport, Economy and Society in Britain, 1750–1914*
    ISBN 0 521 57217 7 (hardback) 0 521 57655 5 (paperback)
34. R. W. Davies, *Soviet Economic Development from Lenin to Khrushchev*
    ISBN 0 521 66260 3 (hardback) 0 521 62742 7 (paperback)
35. H. V. Bowen, *War and British Society, 1688–1815*
    ISBN 0 521 57226 6 (hardback) 0 521 57645 8 (paperback)
36. M. M. Smith, *Debating Slavery: Economy and Society in the Antebellum American South*
    ISBN 0 521 57158 8 (hardback) 0 521 57696 2 (paperback)
37. M. Sanderson, *Education and Economic Decline in Britain, 1870 to the 1990s*
    ISBN 0 521 58170 2 (hardback) 0 521 58842 1 (paperback)
38. V. Berridge, *Health Policy, Health and Society, 1939 to the 1990s*
    ISBN 0 521 57230 4 (hardback) 0 521 57641 5 (paperback)
39. M. E. Mate, *Women in Medieval English Society*
    ISBN 0 521 58322 5 (hardback) 0 521 58733 6 (paperback)
40. P. J. Richardson, *Economic Change in China, c. 1800–1950*
    ISBN 0 521 58396 9 (hardback) 0 521 63571 3 (paperback)
41. J. E. Archer, *Social Unrest and Popular Protest in England, 1780–1840*
    ISBN 0 521 57216 9 (hardback) 0 521 57656 3 (paperback)

42. K. Morgan, *Slavery, Atlantic Trade and the British Economy, 1660–1800*
   ISBN 0 521 58213 X (hardback) 0 521 58814 6 (paperback)
43. C. W. Chalklin, *The Rise of the English Town, 1650–1850*
   ISBN 0 521 66141 2 (hardback) 0 521 66737 2 (paperback)

Previously published as
Studies in Economic and Social History

Titles in the series available from the Macmillan Press Limited:

Economic History Society

The Economic History Society, which numbers around 3,000 members, publishes the quarterly *Economic History Review* (free to members) and holds an annual conference. Enquiries about membership should be addressed to The Assistant Secretary, Economic History Society, PO Box 70, Kingswood, Bristol BS15 5TB. Full-time students may join at special rates.